DELIVER UNFORGETTABLE PRESENTATIONS

"Words have the power to change the direction of your life. When those words are crafted and delivered in the right way the presentation becomes Unforgettable. Three of the most accomplished speakers in the world ... read again, 'in the world,' have written this guide for you to master the power of unforgettable presentations. Follow their advice and let's change the world!"

JIM CATHCART, CSP, CPAE, GOLDEN GAVEL AWARD 2001, SPEAKER HALL OF FAME 1985, AUTHOR OF 21 BOOKS INCLUDING SPEAKING SECRETS OF THE MASTERS

"Deliver Unforgettable Presentations is not another how to map from another "supposed expert" purporting to know how to help you! No, in a global world of noise, Deliver Unforgettable Presentations is the light on the horizon that gives you clarity, confidence and direction to elevate and accelerate your success by three of the true global leaders in the speaking industry. Patricia Fripp, Darren LaCroix, and Mark Brown, are true leaders among leaders. I have known them for more than two-decades and it does not surprise me that everyone quotes them. Learn their insights, methods and understand why CEO's hire them to up their game."

DR. JEFFREY MAGEE, CMC, CBE, CSP, PDM, AUTHOR 20 BOOKS, THREE COLLEGE GRADUATE MANAGEMENT TEXTBOOKS, FOUR BESTSELLERS, AND IS THE PUBLISHER OF PERFORMANCE MAGAZINE

"This book provides you with a short cut to success. Whether you're starting a business or running one, nothing will provide you with a faster shortcut to success than this book. In my experience, nothing will elevate your business faster than having the tools to be a good speaker. The confidence you can get when you know what you're doing when you take the platform can be life changing."

MITZI PERDUE (MRS. FRANK PERDUE), BUSINESSWOMAN, SPEAKER, AUTHOR OF *TOUGH MAN, TENDER CHICKEN* AND *HOW TO MAKE YOUR FAMILY BUSINESS LAST*

"You are never going to find such a usable book on how to deliver an unforgettable presentation anywhere. So, you might as well get this one! The authors give you a step-by-step procedure to start your speech, with engaging and multiple examples to illustrate the seven steps that make up this book from start to finish. Whether you are a beginning speaker with nervous knocking knees when you stand in front of a group or someone who has been delivering presentations for years, you are going to refine your approach. I guarantee it. As a speaker for decades around the globe, I am stunned by the depth and detail of the authors' message. If you are delivering a make-or-break business sales pitch, a celebratory speech, or a simple start to a meeting—you will find what you need in this book. It's also the kind of book where you can skip around, practice some of the ideas you encounter, and then go back and restudy the approach. This little book may become your best lifetime speaking friend."

JANELLE BARLOW, PHD, AUTHOR OF FOUR BOOKS INCLUDING BESTSELLER *A COMPLAINT IS A GIFT*

How To Speak To Be
Remembered And Repeated
In-Person, Online,
And Onstage

DELIVER
UNFORGETTABLE
PRESENTATIONS

PATRICIA FRIPP,
DARREN LACROIX,
AND MARK BROWN

INDIE BOOKS
INTERNATIONAL

ISBN-13: 978-1-957651-06-4

Library of Congress Control Number: 2022904251

Designed by Indie Books International

INDIE BOOKS INTERNATIONAL®, INC.

2424 VISTA WAY, SUITE 316

OCEANSIDE, CA 92054

www.indiebooksintl.com

CONTENTS

Meet The Authors 7

PART I Really? Why Speaking Is Critical To Your Business, Career, and Reputation. 9

PART II Seven Steps To Deliver Unforgettable Presentations 25

Step #1 – Finding Your Content .27
Discover The Treasure Trove Of Your Life

Step #2 – Clarity, Clarity, Clarity 45
Simplify And Demystify Your Process

Step #3 – Structure This! 59
The Skeleton Under The Flesh Of Your Words

Step #4 – Create Your Strong Opening. 73
Open To Arouse Interest In Your Subject

Step #5 – Create Your Compelling Close 85
Close To Reinforce Your Premise And Inspire Action

Step #6 – Make It Unforgettable. 97
How To Be Remembered And Repeated (Speak To The Audience Of Your Audience)

Step #7 – Own Your Stage 111
Prepare Like A Pro For Primetime

PART III What's Next 123

Bonus Step: How You Can Wow Your Audience In Virtual Presentations. 125

Conclusion: Looking Into Your Future. 131

Appendix:
Acknowledgments 135
About The Authors 139

Meet The Three Authors

I N 2001, AT the Toastmasters International convention, Darren LaCroix heard Hall of Fame keynote speaker, Patricia Fripp, describe the Fripp Speech Model, and he thought it was brilliant. Two days later, he beat out 25,000 other speakers to become the 2001 World Champion of Public Speaking. Mark Brown, the 1995 World Champion, was his coach. Since then, these three have collaborated on many public speaking related ventures. This book is an example of how they help their clients and audiences of ambitious professionals like you become unforgettable to their audiences. In their own way, they are legends in the speaking industry.

PART I

Really? Why Speaking Is Critical To Your Business, Career, And Reputation

I T NEVER CEASES to amaze us three authors that intelligent, well-educated, and ambitious professionals frequently overlook developing the number-one skill guaranteed to position them ahead of the crowd. Namely, developing the ability to stand up and speak eloquently in public, or at least stagger to their feet and say anything at all.

What is it about public speaking that terrifies so many? Most likely, it is because we do not want to look, feel, or sound stupid in front of others.

Co-author Patricia Fripp says, "I frequently hear, 'I am a terrible public speaker.'" To which she replies, "No. You are an untrained speaker." Her second comment is always, "Stop telling yourself what you do not want. This is reinforcing what you are going to change."

You improve what you focus on. Fripp tells her coaching clients, "You have invested your entire career training to be a competent CPA, engineer, nurse, dentist, financial advisor, or content expert."

For decades, we have focused on how to get your message across in a more clear, concise, and interesting way that brings more buy-in for your ideas and *makes you unforgettable.*

Anyone can stand in front of an audience or behind a webcam and deliver a presentation. Each presentation you deliver enhances or lowers your reputation. We encourage you to develop the knowledge and skills to become unforgettable every time you present.

We assure you, becoming a great public speaker and presenter who delivers unforgettable presentations is not rocket science. However, it is more complex than most professionals realize.

What you will learn from this book are timeless techniques and proven principles that, when adopted, will increase the likelihood of becoming unforgettable. You may find them surprisingly simple. However, they are often little-known and frequently overlooked.

No matter your career or personal goals, mastering public speaking skills is an important part of your personal development.

When co-author Mark Brown worked at *Reader's Digest* in the 1990s, job openings were posted on a notice board outside the cafeteria. Positions included chief information officer, staff accountant, mailroom assistant, and everything in between. Every job description, without exception, had a single common denominator: *"Excellent verbal and written communication skills required."*

If your goal is to be a full-time paid professional speaker, great. If you're a business professional who wants to advance your career, these skills will give you a competitive advantage. If you're an ambitious entrepreneur, you probably realized that the least expensive way to promote your business is to showcase your expertise by delivering interesting, compelling talks to audiences filled with potential clients. If you are a leader, you will learn to inspire action and commitment from your associates, partners, and customers.

You are smart enough to realize improving communication skills is helpful in almost every area of your life. The higher up the corporate ladder you go, the more critical your presentation skills become.

Early in your career, you will get promoted faster when you act, dress, and speak for the position you want, not have.

We know you're busy. Therefore, we designed this step-by-step book to make it easier for you to create your unforgettable presentation, whether your goal is to speak professionally, advance your career, or promote your business.

Consider a few of the benefits of mastering public speaking, which will encourage you to get out of your comfort zone and take action.

DEVELOPING GOOD PUBLIC SPEAKING SKILLS WILL IMPROVE YOUR POTENTIAL FOR PROFESSIONAL GROWTH AND OPPORTUNITIES.

Patricia's good friend Steve Gerardi has always loved rock music. At age fifteen, at his first rock show, he watched the promoter's team walking around the arena, and Steve said to his friend, "This is what I am going to do," even though he did not know exactly what it entailed.

In Indianapolis, the local production company was Sunshine Promotions. He began as a part-time showrunner with the goal of being a concert production manager and talent buyer.

After two years, the call came. Gerardi was offered a full-time job so he dropped everything else and moved back to Indianapolis.

Lucky for Steve, his last boss had encouraged and helped finance all employees who wanted to attend the Dale Carnegie Public Speaking Course.

Steve took advantage of the opportunity and excelled. Afterward, he told his friends, "It was amazing how fast being able to stand up and talk to strangers built my confidence, and my skills increased very quickly."

After Steve had been working for Sunshine for eighteen months, his boss asked Steve to come to his office. He handed him two pages of handwritten notes and said, "Please read this. Do you understand it? Tell me what you think it says."

Steve confidently replied, "You say it is imperative for success in our industry to re-negotiate and create deals with concert venues. Especially when tickets are not selling as we expected. Even with a signed contract, there are times we have to be flexible and renegotiate."

Steve's boss and his partner were shy, and neither liked the spotlight. Even though Steve was the newest and youngest employee, he was the only one the boss trusted to speak on behalf of Sunshine Promotions.

That night, Steve was on a plane and flew to another state to attend and speak at a regional meeting of venue managers.

Steve recalled, "Even though I was the youngest person in the room, once I finished speaking, everyone there treated me as an industry expert. This built my confidence and credibility, and the relationships were very good for Sunshine."

Eleven years later, when the boss and his partner sold the company for $65 million, Steve was ready to open his own company.

As the president of SG Entertainment, Steve helps companies book entertainment for their corporate events and celebrations.

DEVELOPING GOOD PUBLIC SPEAKING SKILLS WILL BOOST YOUR CONFIDENCE IN FRONT OF YOUR SENIOR MANAGEMENT.

Will Strickland is a staff performance engineer at Nutanix. Like many brilliant technical experts, they invest years developing their skills and suddenly find themselves pushed more into the spotlight. Strickland sent Patricia an email saying, "Four months ago, I attended your presentation skills class. I felt compelled to let you know how insanely helpful that course has been for me. For as long as I can remember, I've been a very anxious public speaker. After your class, my anxiety seems to have magically melted away. Recently, I delivered an hour-long talk to my twenty-five-person team. The audience included management, a director, and our technical director.

"Thanks to your presentation skills class, I felt at ease the entire time. It was a technical subject, so it could have been dry and boring. The techniques you taught kept coming back to my mind. There is no way to tell you how wonderful it was to receive many kudos, including from the technical director who wrote, 'Congratulations. Great stories and analysis. You really do have to speak more often.' Thank you very much for the class; it was an amazing experience!"

DEVELOPING GOOD PUBLIC SPEAKING SKILLS HELPS YOU MAKE MORE SALES, MORE OFTEN.

To sell, you need technical skills, product knowledge, a sound relationship management system, to understand how you compare to your competition, discipline, persistence, and good organization skills. However, these alone will not make you successful in sales. Once your work pays off, and you have an initial conversation or more formal presentation with a prospect, you need to know what to say and why what you say will be persuasive and compelling. Often, the best presentation wins the business.

Powerful, persuasive presentation skills give you a competitive advantage over your competition.

Earlier in her career, when Patricia was primarily a keynote speaker, a large food service company invited her to keynote their yearly sales conference. After her speech, Jennifer, the national sales manager, pulled her aside and said, "I liked your speech. However, I really loved how you delivered it. Can you teach our salespeople to speak that way? We sell quality food and uniforms to hospitals and healthcare systems. It takes us a year of work and relationship development for us to be in a position to deliver an hour presentation to a hospital board. It is worth $9 million a year if we win the business. We are losing sales, and it has nothing to do with our offering or price. When I follow up, I keep hearing the presentation skills of our competitors are better than ours."

As Fripp put together the program for them, little did she know Jennifer had just given her the secret to always being in demand, no matter how good or bad the economy is.

Lucky for them and Fripp, Jennifer realized that she could improve the presentation skills of her sales team for a relatively small investment.

Why do so many companies assume their seasoned content experts and sales teams can naturally deliver any message well? Many well-educated professionals have never received any training or coaching in presentation skills and don't take the initiative themselves. Often, it is because they had a bad experience.

Shelly Seeger read Patricia's special report on *Eleven Mistakes Sales Professionals Make in Their Presentations* and called. She said, "Help! I work with a large software company, and we only hire seasoned sales professionals. They must have at least ten years of experience selling technology. Naturally, we assumed they could successfully tell our company story. Until we had a meeting and all the sales professionals had to deliver in front of our leadership team. The leaders were horrified! They have charged me to search the globe for the best sales presentation skills team. Lucky for us, you are only thirty-eight miles from headquarters."

DEVELOPING GOOD PUBLIC SPEAKING SKILLS HELPS YOU SOUND CLEAR, CONCISE, AND CREDIBLE.

Its dedication drives the American Payroll Association to the education and elevation of its members. Every year the APA delivers hundreds of training courses, online presentations, and in-person and virtual conferences. Their visionary Executive Director Dan Maddux hires celebrities, hall-of-fame keynote speakers, bestselling authors, and government experts to deliver main stage presentations. Dan realized his elected association leaders, APA award winners, and the dozens of payroll-related breakout session speakers must follow or share the stage with these luminaries. Naturally, they felt the pressure. For two decades, Dan and the APA have invested in presentation skills training and coaching for his leaders and all APA speakers.

The feedback the APA receives from each evaluation confirms presentation skills training is a wise investment for the APA.

Many members never dreamed they would look out at an audience one day with over two thousand people sitting looking up at them. The APA members feel inspired when they see their peers and friends doing so well. The APA speakers find the presentation training elevates them in their own companies and careers. No wonder while other associations may be losing members, the APA is always exceptionally healthy.

At a recent international payroll conference, Dan was asked, "How come your APA speakers are always the best in our industry?" Dan replied, "We have a commitment to, and a budget for, presentation skills training and coaching for all our speakers. They consider this training a non-taxable fringe benefit that helps them excel in their own careers."

DEVELOPING GOOD PUBLIC SPEAKING SKILLS IS THE BEST WAY TO PROMOTE YOUR PRODUCT, SERVICE, OR COMPANY.

Before Patricia became a professional speaker and executive speech coach, she was San Francisco's number-one men's hairstylist with a swanky salon in the Financial District. Her clients were ambitious professionals and movers and shakers in business. She found it exhilarating to develop relationships with titans of business. It was a great education in business, and many of the relationships she developed helped launch her speaking career.

On weekends, she travelled around the country, demonstrating the latest men's hairstyling techniques and delivering management, motivation, and sales seminars to hairstylists for a hair product company.

Her clients in the salon began to say, "Come and speak to my Golden Gate Breakfast Club," or, "My Rotary Club would enjoy hearing your message about good customer service," and then, "Would you like to speak at our team meeting?"

After two talks, she realized this was the least expensive and a fun way to advertise her salon and drive more business for her stylists. Before long, she delivered at least two talks a week, and it paid dividends.

One of her clients was Peter Butler. He was in the financial services business, in his fifties, and trained for the Ironman Triathlon. Peter found it such a life-changing experience that he continued to get involved with various interesting marathons in wonderful and often exotic places. Patricia asked him if he would like to speak to her professional women's organization. He accepted and began his presentation this way.

"Training for a triathlon is very much like planning your financial future."

For the next twenty-five minutes, he regaled his audience of eighty professional women with his funny and challenging experiences. In the last four minutes, he reviewed the lessons he had learned from his adventures and tied his message back to planning for a sound financial future.

He said, "These are the four questions you need to answer and discuss with your financial advisor," then closed with an inspiring thought. The audience leaped to their feet, applauding. As the meeting closed, dozens were in line asking for his card.

From this first successful experience, Peter, like Patricia, let it be known he was open to speaking to any interested group. Neither delivered a sales presentation about their services. Both gave interesting, entertaining, and thought-provoking talks that gave them visibility, the opportunity to become objects of interest to their audiences, and they drove business.

Developing a talk to deliver in your community builds new relationships. People do business with those they know, like, and find interesting. With so many organizations meeting virtually, you can expand your vision of local. This is the best way to promote your product, service, or company.

MEMORABLE PRESENTATIONS

Memorable presentations can help you:

- Increase your influence in helping others make decisions.
- Inspire action and commitment in your team.
- Get buy-in for your ideas and recommendations.
- Gain the trust and respect of others.
- Prove you are sincere, authentic, and reliable.
- Build new relationships.
- Expand your professional network.

Overall, speaking at events and conferences is a good way to build credibility. The more well-known the event, the better, as you can add these speaking achievements to your resume.

PUBLIC SPEAKING CAN ALSO HELP YOU STAND OUT AT WORK.

When you learn to speak up in meetings, promote your ideas, and present yourself as a professional, your opportunities for advancement increase. Effective speaking skills can also help you excel in job interviews.

PUBLIC SPEAKING CAN SIGNIFICANTLY BOOST YOUR CONFIDENCE.

Overcoming the fears and insecurities that accompany public speaking is empowering. Furthermore, connecting with audiences can be a strong reminder that you have valuable insights and opinions to share with the world.

YOUR CONFIDENCE LEVELS WILL GROW AS YOU GO FROM SPEAKING TO SMALL GROUPS TO LARGE AUDIENCES.

This skill will benefit you not just on stage but also in everyday life, whether in a meeting or a social gathering.

Another benefit of public speaking is that you will suddenly find that everyone wants to talk with you when you speak at a company meeting or an event. This is a valuable opportunity to make friends, build business contacts, and generate business.

Sean, the brilliant lead counsel of a large biotech company, received an award for leadership given by a powerful women's organization in his industry. He was the first man to receive this award in their twenty-five-year history. He had always been a champion for diversity and inclusion for decades before it was a popular topic of conversation. Sean is a shy, modest man, with hundreds of lawyers reporting to him.

When he first met with Patricia, he said, "I warn you, I am a reluctant client. I only accept speeches to talk about the law, and how on earth can I fill twenty-five minutes talking about diversity and inclusion?" Before he left his coaching session, he asked, "How soon can we meet again?" Patricia watched his presentation, and he was truly magnificent. Later, he reported to a mutual friend, "I could not believe it; thirty people came up afterward and wanted to have lunch and get to know me."

These benefits are more easily obtained when you deliver unforgettable presentations. This book is designed to show you how.

We are going to take you through our proven seven-step process. It has been honed over decades at our workshops and with one-on-one coaching. This process will help you create better presentations more quickly. You may find it takes some effort; becoming world-class at any endeavor usually does. We have simplified the process to save you time. Once you master the process, it will become instinctive and help you deliver remembered and repeated presentations. Are you ready? Let's get started.

PART II

Seven Steps
To Deliver
Unforgettable
Presentations

STEP #1

Finding Your Content

*"We respect the position. We fight in
the streets for the person."*
Patricia Fripp

BEGIN BY DISCOVERING the treasure trove of your life. If you are just getting started as a presenter, you may feel as we did. *What the heck am I going to talk about?* Congratulations, you are human. You may be thinking, *I'm not an expert on anything.*

As one of the first women in a male-dominated industry, co-author Patricia learned to take advantage of the opportunity that her expertise presented. How do you now make a living? What do you know that you currently take for granted that others would like to know? What have you studied or have a true passion for? What do others ask your opinion or guidance on?

Begin with any area or topic where you know more than others.

As a successful entrepreneur in the early days when men's hairstyling was a new industry, Patricia realized she knew how to build a small or medium-sized business. A hair product company engaged her to travel to different regions of the US to demonstrate haircutting techniques and teach other stylists "How to Get, Keep, and Deserve Customers." The clients in San Francisco's Financial District were influential and successful. They invited her to speak to their service clubs and team meetings.

As Patricia's skills and reputation grew, so did her clientele because of her relationships with the people sitting in a hairstyling chair. Having access to so many brilliant minds helped her develop a repertoire of stories and business case histories.

Patricia frequently asked her hairstyling clients, "What made you the best salesperson in your company? What did your small company do that attracted a large company who wanted to buy it?"

Clients, co-workers, and connections you make can be a great source of interesting information and great wisdom. Your life experience and relationships can provide great content for your unforgettable presentation.

Being unforgettable comes from a combination of engaging content, an organized flow, well-crafted words delivered with your personality, and style of delivery.

Your best content, stories, and life lessons will come from your life experiences. Your audience will relate to you as they see themselves in some of the personal stories. These stories will come from your personal and professional life.

How often have you watched a masterful presenter tell a magnificent story that mesmerizes the audience? Did you secretly have "story envy"? You are not alone.

What you listened to was not their first telling. The first time they told their story, it might have been interesting. However, what mesmerized you is the result of their process to polish that story. The technique is not complicated.

When co-author Darren first started coaching with co-author Mark, he handed him the first draft of his speech. Mark noticed what was missing. He asked Darren, "Have you had any failures in your life that you can draw from?"

"Yes, a business failure," Darren replied.

Mark said, "That's perfect."

Nine years before, Darren had written his failure as a joke for an exercise in a comedy writing book. Here he was working on the most important speech of his life, and he hadn't even considered a story that had powerful content. We all have content that we may have never considered, and this chapter is designed to help you find your content. Later, we will show you how to organize and polish it.

Mark also told Darren, "Think about a special child in your life. If you had only *one opportunity* to leave that child with *one life lesson*, what would it be? Don't answer immediately.

Go back over your life, invest some time to find the most important lesson that you would share, and get back to me in a few days."

Mark inspired Darren to reflect on his life and the lessons he had learned. Darren was on a content-finding mission. That was a simple but significant exercise, and average presenters will not invest the time to do this.

Some of your content you will use frequently. Other for specific occasions. Some to open meetings and entertain your team members. In a later chapter, you will learn how to customize your presentations for particular audiences.

Commit to the content-finding process. This exercise is crucial and will lay the foundation for the rest of the steps. Once you realize that great content and ideas to build on are everywhere, keep adding ideas. Be aware; always have a way to record or write your thoughts down. As you know, ideas come at random moments.

Even if you have no idea how you can develop a thought into content, write it down.

How do you capture your idea? Any way that works for you.

Start a story file. It's a simple concept. If you owned a furniture store, your inventory would be furniture. If you owned a flooring store, your inventory would be flooring. You are a presenter; your inventory is stories.

You want to make your story file searchable. Whether you use your favorite app or a simple Word document, it doesn't matter. You choose. What matters is that you are familiar with the format, and you constantly add to it. Before you go to bed, mentally review your day for any new thoughts, ideas, and experiences.

These are your stories; they are easier to deliver because they are yours. Right now, you are in the mining mode.

Through our decades of coaching experience, we've learned it's much easier to authentically tell your stories than to repeat those from others.

You have more content inside you than you know or ever thought. The following "content developing questions" come directly from our executive coaching sessions. The secret is to start at the beginning of your life and revisit where your values, influences, and natural inclinations were developed.

We recommend you read the first ten questions, pause, and add your ideas to your story file. At this point, we intend to jog your memory and help you realize the value of your experiences that other people can learn from.

It may be easier for you to collaborate on this exercise with a like-minded friend. We are with you in spirit; however, if you would benefit from a co-creator and sounding board, invite them. Patricia always reminds presenters, "It is *very difficult* to be *creative in isolation.*"

The statement we most frequently hear is, "I want to be a speaker, but I have no idea what to talk about." You have our guarantee upon completion of this content-developing exercise, you will never say that again. Expect your head to hurt, and you will suddenly realize so many of the principles and experiences of your life are universal. You will discover you are a lot more interesting than you realize, and future audiences are waiting to hear your message.

We have different categories of questions, separated into the following three sections:

1. Universal Questions—All presenters can benefit from these.

2. Corporate Speaker Questions—These are used to generate content for any business-related presentations, both internal and external.

3. Entrepreneur Questions—These are designed to find content for your marketing presentations.

We have broken this process down for you to come back and easily reference.

FIRST CATEGORY: UNIVERSAL QUESTIONS

In case you believe you have little to say, here is a checklist of questions to consider:

✓ Where were you born?

✓ What was that city/town known for?

✓ What did your parents do?

✓ What advice did they give you that you still remember?

✓ Who were your best childhood friends?

✓ What did you love to do together?

✓ What are your best childhood memories?

✓ Were you interested in sports? If so, what sports?

✓ What were your extracurricular activities? Band? Debate team? Chorus?

✓ Did your grandparents influence you? School teachers? Coaches?

✓ Did your minister influence you? Piano teacher? Scout leader?

✓ If yes, what was their advice?

✓ What lessons did they teach you that you still rely on today?

✓ How did they help develop your character?

✓ What actions have you taken because of their influence?

✓ As an adult, what stories do you vividly remember, and can repeat, word for word, that you heard from your parents? Grandparents? Uncles and aunts?

✓ What favorite stories do your family share at family gatherings?

✓ If you went to college, what friends, professors, events are still memorable?

✓ What companies have you worked for?

✓ Please go through the timeline of your job experience. Start with your first job, such as being a waitress or paperboy at twelve. What did you learn from that?

✓ Make a list of every manager you remember and ask yourself, "What did I learn from them (good or bad)?" Remember, you can learn what not to do from a bad boss.

✓ Reflecting on your career, what were the high points? The biggest successes? The greatest failures?

✓ With each job you held, what amusing, dramatic, or poignant stories did you come home and tell your family or friends?

✓ What have been your favorite hobbies?

✓ Who have been your mentors and role models?

✓ What did they tell you that you have never forgotten?

✓ What have you done with their advice?

✓ What have been your best vacations? Why? What happened? Who did you meet?

✓ Are you still friends?

✓ Do you and your spouse/partner/family have different memories of favorite vacations?

✓ What charity or community involvement is important? Why?

✓ How about Special Olympics? Junior Achievement?

✓ Your favorite charities?

✓ What stories from these experiences do you find memorable?

✓ What stories have you told that when you are at a social gathering, one of your friends always says, "Hey _____, tell them the story of when _____."

✓ As a consumer, what experiences best reflect incredible customer service?

✓ As a consumer, what experiences best reflect bad customer service?

✓ What salespeople have most effectively sold to you?

✓ What salespeople didn't get the sale because they didn't earn the right to receive your money?

✓ What have been your major investments? Home? Car? Wedding? What stories do you remember *about the sales process?*

DELIVER UNFORGETTABLE PRESENTATIONS

✓ Why did you choose to do business with *these* sales professionals?

✓ Who in history, living or dead, would you most like to meet, and why?

✓ Who is your favorite entertainer? Actor? Artist? Why? How has their contribution to society affected you?

✓ What do you go home and complain about?

✓ If you were going to live your life again knowing what you now know, how would you do it differently?

✓ If you were going to start your career again, knowing what you now know, what different choices would you make?

✓ Do you consider your life or career a success? If yes, what are the lessons for others?

✓ Who are your most interesting friends and acquaintances?

✓ What stories have you heard them tell that you can't wait to retell others?

✓ What adversities and challenges have you overcome and how?

✓ What are your brushes with fame? What did you learn?

✓ What do you now know that a few years ago, you couldn't imagine knowing?

✓ What now is commonplace that ten years ago, you would not have thought possible?

✓ What do you now automatically do that you once struggled to learn?

✓ What do your friends and family tease you about?

✓ What personal accomplishment are you most proud of? (Do not say your family.)

✓ Choose a child in your life. If you had only one opportunity to leave that child with one lesson from your life experience to help them through the rest of their life, what would it be?

SECOND CATEGORY: CORPORATE PRESENTER QUESTIONS

These are used to generate content for internal meetings and client events.

Business presentations include team, regional, divisional, and all-hands meetings. Then the terrifying report to senior management, project updates, requests for funding, client conversations, and technical demonstrations. Next, the yearly sales meetings, presenting at industry events, and trade show demonstrations. Leaders, marketing professionals, engineers, and IT experts deliver keynotes, interviews, panel discussions, and technical presentations.

Many of these presentations include customer case histories and the company origin story. The following questions will be a guide to help you have an arsenal of stories in your back pocket when you need them. Here is a checklist of questions:

- ✓ Who founded your company and its philosophy?

- ✓ What have been milestones, challenges, innovations, changes, and greatest successes during your company history?

- ✓ How does your competition perceive you?

- ✓ How do you compare to your competition?

- ✓ What is "a day in the life" for your audience?

- ✓ What do your employees do superbly well and worthy of congratulations?

- ✓ What was your experience, and how did you feel on your first day on the job?

> **"Your audience wants to hear you; they also want to know you."**
>
> MARK BROWN

- ✓ What did your boss say when you were first promoted?

- ✓ When you were a child, what did you want to grow up and be?

✓ On reflection, what was the moment you realized you were destined to do what you are now doing?

✓ What stories have you heard at the water cooler? Coffee pot? Cafeteria? Did you go home and tell your family about them?

THIRD CATEGORY: ENTREPRENEUR QUESTIONS

These are helpful with marketing presentations.

Every entrepreneur experiences ups and downs.

Delivering presentations to your local community increases your visibility and credibility. If your product or service is national or international in-scope, virtual presentations and adding to social media will enhance your reach.

Through your personal stories, audience members feel they know you and are more likely to build trust in you. Trust is critical to develop professional relationships.

Here is a checklist of questions:

✓ When was the moment you realized you needed to go into business for yourself?

✓ What advice did your father/mother give you that applies to your business?

✓ At social events, what are the five most frequently asked questions about your business or profession?

✓ What are the personal or business challenges/ problems that you or your company solves?

✓ Who are your five most satisfied clients? Taking one at a time, how has your product or service changed their condition?

✓ How have your satisfied clients articulated how they feel about your product or service?

✓ What did you accidentally do that paid dividends?

✓ What did you intentionally do that was a great decision?

✓ What were your greatest hiring successes and failures? What was the lesson?

✓ What amusing stories from your business do you entertain your friends with?

✓ What key idea do you want your audience to know about your business?

✓ Is there a connection between you, your business, or your family and your audience?

BONUS: HIGH-LEVEL EXECUTIVE QUESTIONS

Working with brilliant, high-level executives is exhilarating and an awesome responsibility, simply because of the importance and impact of their words. The challenge is that they are so busy, and it is difficult to find enough time. Each situation is different. However, what you have already learned also applies to high-level executive presentations.

Patricia is an awarding-winning speaker and speechwriter. Most of her sessions begin with two questions: "Please give me a snapshot of your life and career." Then, "If you had one sentence rather than forty-five minutes, what would you say?"

Here is a checklist of questions:

- ✓ If you had one sentence rather than forty-five minutes, what would you say?
- ✓ Can you please give me a snapshot of your life?
- ✓ When was the first time you realized the importance of strategy?
- ✓ Who has been your greatest influence?
- ✓ As a young person, what was your greatest aspiration?
- ✓ At what point in your career did you realize you were exceptional?
- ✓ What has been your greatest challenge in selling to your board of directors?
- ✓ What will your audience be thinking before you walk on stage?
- ✓ Specifically, what do you want your audience to do because of your presentation?
- ✓ How does your message fit from a historical perspective?

✓ What legacy do you want to leave?

✓ How do you explain corporate citizenship to your children?

✓ Corporately, what are you most proud of?

✓ Personally, what are you most proud of?

✓ At dinner parties, what stories do you find yourself most frequently telling?

At this point, we trust you will not make the mistake of invalidating your own life experience. You have plenty to say, and our goal is to help you say it well.

COMMON MISTAKES AT THIS STEP

Mistake #1:
Neglecting to look for the life lessons from your experiences.

Mistake #2:
Invalidating your life experience. Thinking other people's content is more important than yours.

STEP #1 ACTIVITIES

Step #1 Activity #1
If you have not already done so, start your story file.

Step #1 Activity #2
Review the questions, and find which resonate most.

Step #1 Activity #3
Every day, tell three friends one of your stories triggered by one of the previous questions.

Think about it this way: If you owned a bookstore, your inventory would be books. You are a presenter, and your inventory includes stories, case studies, and metaphors. Your story file is the place you will draw from. It is the gold from your life. Keep adding to it for the rest of your career.

If you make this a new habit, you will be able to quickly create better presentations.

Congratulations, you have completed Step #1, finding your content, the toughest part of the process.

This is the most involved and most energy-consuming step. The work you do here will make the other steps easier and faster and your presentation more powerful. Now, on to Step #2: clarity.

Clarity, Clarity, Clarity

"Context provides clarity."
Mark Brown

OUR NEXT STEP is to simplify and demystify your process for you.

Now that you understand the *why* and have mined your life and understand the *abundance of content* available to you, we can get to the structure. This is how you organize your presentation with a logical flow. It will be easy for you and your audience to remember with minimal or no notes.

The more you work on clarifying your content, organizing your structure, then adding some initial scripting, the easier it will be for you to have a professional-sounding delivery.

You would not build a home without a blueprint. You would not drive to another city without a map, GPS, or good directions. It is the same with your speech structure. It is what we consider the *skeleton under the flesh* of your words.

Once you have decided on the content to include in your presentation, you are ready to learn how to organize it into a strong structure.

The first step is to clarify the intent and benefit of your message for the audience.

To simplify this process, think of a presentation you must deliver shortly, or revisit one you have already given, and look at it with fresh eyes.

Look at your content list, and select what will go into this presentation. It will most likely include your key ideas, stories, examples, statistics, and quotes from authorities. If you are presenting at somebody else's meeting, listen to the project champion or person in charge. Perhaps they would like you to reinforce meeting themes or contribute topics of specific interest to them.

Who is your audience? What is the purpose of your presentation? Based on your subject, what do you want them to *know, feel,* and *do*?

This process will also help you gain clarity into your thinking and message.

CLARIFYING YOUR CENTRAL THEME OR PREMISE

Your first step in creating your speech structure is to answer this question: "Based on my subject, what is my premise or central theme?" This is the big idea you want to get across.

Every TV show, movie, and book has a clear premise. So does your presentation.

Every audience wants to know that you *know who they are*. The premise statement is valuable because your core presentation helps you adapt your focus and examples for each audience. Sometimes you state your premise. Other times, it is in the back of your mind, motivating your presentation.

Imagine that we ask you, "If you had one sentence rather than forty-five minutes for your presentation, what would you say?"

If your answer is in one sentence and not a paragraph, you probably have your central theme. That is the premise of your presentation.

Once you have your premise, list your key talking points—what we like to call your *points of wisdom*—into the outline of your presentation. Your talking points prove your premise; they make your case for you.

The *Fripp Premise Formula* will help you clarify your thinking and organize your content around it, while connecting to your specific audience.

Grab your pad, and write *down* the page, not across it:

Every . . .

Can . . . the subject or result of your talk.

Underneath that, write "How?" and your three *points of wisdom:*

How?

    1.

    2.

    3.

At this point, you are thinking, *That is what I want; how do I do that?* We answer the burning question we led you to ask based on the premise statement.

The premise of this book, and any presentation we deliver on this subject, is the following:
Every ambitious professional or leader can create an unforgettable presentation.

THE PREMISE STATEMENT

Every (fill in the blank) can (fill in subject or result):

- Every entrepreneur *can* build their business and credibility.
- Every sales professional *can* drive more sales with their existing database.
- Every leader *can* inspire action and commitment.
- Every educator *can* actively engage their students.

THE PREMISE FORMULA LEADS TO THE *POINTS OF WISDOM*. THIS IS THE SIMPLE STRUCTURE WHERE YOU ADD YOUR INFORMATION.

Every . . .

Can . . . the subject or result of your talk.

Underneath that, write "How?" and your three *points of wisdom*:

How?

    1.

    2.

    3.

These are your *points of wisdom* developed into chunks of content.

For example, Patricia worked with the president of a $2 billion technology company that aspired to become a $20 billion company. The *purpose* of this presentation was to communicate to the audience, "You are at the right place at the right time, and our strategy is sound."

Patricia's instructions were, "Our president is brilliant and not a bad speaker. He is an engineer and very modest. We want you to write him a speech, and make him look like a rockstar presenter. You have four hours."

After "Good morning, sir," she asked her first question: "If you had one sentence rather than forty-five minutes for your presentation, what would you say?" Our executive's reply: "This is a brand-new company."

Executives usually have little time, so Patricia asks questions and helps frame their conversations into the logical flow of the presentation. Her goal, and ours, is to create a conversational presentation. It is difficult for most people to sit down and write a speech that sounds conversational. Patricia's recommendation is to tighten, dramatize, and add specific language that sounds like you normally speak.

Our executive was talking about the strategy that would help them get there. Patricia asked, "When did you first realize the importance of strategy?"

"When I was a fourteen-year-old ball boy before the French Open, I was playing against my best friend, and we were equally matched in talent and experience. His sister was our ball boy. Naturally, she wanted her brother to win and was doing all in her power to sabotage my game. That is when I realized the importance of strategy, when I was equally matched and at a disadvantage."

Many executives ask, "Do they want to hear these personal stories?"

That is when Patricia tells them, "Yes, they respect your position. When they feel they know you as a person, they will fight in the streets for you."

As Mark tells his audiences, "Your audience wants to hear from you. They also want to feel they know you." This was exceptionally important to our executive, as 40 percent of the 1,500-person worldwide sales audience had been acquired through acquisition.

Let us look at our executive's *unspoken* premise: "Every XYZ sales professional *can* do superbly well."

How? Remember, with our acquisition and sound strategy, we are now a new company.

To prove the premise, the structure followed logically, answering the unspoken questions of the audience.

Who . . . decided, and why did they take this bold move?

What . . . is the strategy, and how does it differ from before?

How . . . will this change our impact on the marketplace and our future?

One of the common challenges for this book's authors, when working individually with clients and collectively with coaching camps and seminars, is to help speakers gain clarity for their message when they have plenty to say. Once you focus on *who* the audience is and *the outcome,* this simple yet powerful premise statement and formula give you the skeleton under the flesh of your words.

LET US GO DEEPER INTO HOW YOU PROVE YOUR PREMISE AND DEVELOP YOUR CHUNKS OF CONTENT.

Three *points of wisdom* is a guide based on a strong historical perspective.

The Rule of Three is a writing principle suggesting that a trio of events or characters is more humorous, satisfying, or effective than other numbers. Audiences are more likely to remember information conveyed using The Rule of Three. The three elements provide brevity and rhythm with the smallest amount of information needed to create a pattern. It makes an author or speaker appear knowledgeable while remaining both accessible and catchy.

Slogans, film titles, jokes, speaking techniques, and writing have been structured in threes, a tradition that grew out of oral storytelling—for example, *The Three Little Pigs*, *Three Billy Goats Gruff*, and *The Three Musketeers*. Similarly, adjectives are often grouped in threes to emphasize an idea.

The Latin phrase "Omne trium perfectum" ("Everything that comes in threes is perfect," or "Every set of three is complete") conveys the same idea as The Rule of Three.

Most speakers know the importance of using The Rule of Three, but most of us are unaware of where it came from. We use this ancient mathematical law of proportion in ways we don't even think about. Abraham Lincoln learned about it in his one-room schoolhouse. Even Aristotle, in his *Art of Rhetoric*, referred to "three types of speeches" and "three forms of proof."

Irrespective of its mathematical overtones, the number three is truly magical. Speech coaches insist that people can most easily remember something if it is said three different times. Shakespeare used it in *Julius Ceasar* with "Friends,

Romans, countrymen." Thomas Jefferson used it in The Declaration of Independence with "Life, liberty, and the pursuit of happiness."

US Marine Corps instructors teach that a Marine should limit their attention to three tasks or goals. Comedians often use the rule of three effectively. Their first comment names the topic, the second sets a pattern, and the third unexpectedly switches the pattern, which is funny.

What does it mean for you? Simply that focusing your message on no more than three significant points and repeating them in different ways throughout your presentation is sure to give your presentation maximum impact. Let the classic Rule of Three add power to your writing, storytelling, and presentations.

Points of wisdom can be rhythmic. Alliteration and rhyme are the most common ways to accomplish this.

Mark's *points of wisdom* in his keynote "Celebrate Change" are:

- Change is inevitable.
- Change requires risk.
- Change creates opportunity.

In his keynote "Humor and Hope," Darren's *points of wisdom* were:
- Build belief.
- Become clear.
- Be brave.

Points of wisdom are often definitive, as in Mark's example, or directive, as in Darren's example.

The Fripp Presentation Model has the three ovals to the right of each topic or *point of wisdom* to prove each point. Remember, this is a good guide. With longer programs—for example, two- and three-day training—for each day, you can consider three points before the lunch break and three after. For technical and complex subjects, you will have a topic and subtopics. In these cases, review at the end of topic one, and take questions and answers before you move to the next topic.

A CHUNK OF CONTENT

The Fripp Presentation Model has nine circles representing the content for your three *points of wisdom*. Keep in mind that three is the guideline. After each one, you need a transition line communicating that you have completed that point. We refer to the *points of wisdom*, supporting evidence, and transition line as a *chunk of content*. The model shows that your complete presentation consists of three chunks of content, commonly called *the body of your presentation,* wrapped in your *opening* and *closing*.

YOUR AUDIENCE

In Mark and Darren's live workshops, each participant has a name tent to help the trainers identify them. On the reverse side are cartoon representations of the different personas in our audience. This side faces the workshop attendees to constantly remind them of who may be in their audience. They include:

The Skeptic: Doubts everything

The Source: Wants your sources

The Young Gun: Needs engagement to stay interested

The Veteran: More experienced in the industry than you

The Newbie: Needs clarity, direction, and hope

The Know-it-all: Mistakenly thinks they know everything

The Cheerleader: Loves you and posts about you

WHAT CAN BE INCLUDED IN YOUR *POINTS OF WISDOM*

Here is a list of what can be included in your *points of wisdom*:

Anecdotes: A story about a person or event, usually making the listeners laugh or ponder over a topic.

Analogies: Comparisons between two objects, typically for explanation or clarification. These are useful for explaining abstract or unfamiliar ideas.

Application: How does your topic or suggestion relate to your audience, and what do they do next?

Call to Action: What action do you recommend your audience take next?

Captivating Visuals: Your photos, original images, graphics, and screenshots.

Case Histories: Stories of how your product or service changed your customer's results.

Demonstrations: A product, process, or technical demo. This includes coaching an audience member on a speaking technique you have introduced.

Exercises: Get your audience involved in what they are learning.

Explanation: If you introduce an idea or phrase that is little-known or in a new context, what does it mean?

Illustrations: Includes the use of props or activities.

Interesting Statistics: These can prove the importance of your message or need for your product.

Little-Known Facts: Especially powerful if they are relevant to this specific audience.

Song/Poem/Music/Dance/Magic: If you have a talent that many do not, find a way to incorporate it in your presentations.

Surveys/Polls: Another way to keep the attention of your audience.

Quotes: From authorities, personal quotes not generally known, and audience members you interviewed.

Video Clips: Ideally minimally used or you own them.

Based on your experience, this is a guide that you can add to.

Mistake #1. Thinking your audience is everyone.

Mistake #2. Including your outline in your premise.

Mistake #3. Not staying focused on one point at a time.

Mistake #4. Too many points within one presentation.

Mistake #5. Not varying examples.

STEP #2 ACTIVITY

Create the premise for your presentation. Then write your *points of wisdom* on the left side of the Fripp Presentation Model. Add the stories, statistics, audience application; then write one or two keywords in the ovals that support your *points of wisdom*. If necessary, revisit all the work you did mining your life for experiences.

After that, you are ready to attack structure, which is the focus of the next step.

Structure This!

*"Good structure gives you confidence
and your audience clarity."*
Darren LaCroix

STRUCTURE IS THE skeleton under the flesh of your words.
How often have you sat in an audience and been
mesmerized by a speaker? Was it their compelling
content? Were their stories scintillating? Did they have the
ability to reach out and grab you in a way, and you thought,
Wow, the speaker is talking to me?

Be honest: how many life-changing, career-building, or truly
unforgettable presentations have you heard? Have you ever
been *that* speaker? At this point, you realize what that
ability means to you and your career.

To review: Your content or material is everything that makes
up what you say in your presentation. Your structure is the
order and framework of your presentation.

Your delivery is how you communicate your message, personality, and authority.

These are the elements of your presentations we use for the Fripp Presentation Model:

- ✓ Strong Opening: How you launch into your presentation and engage the audience.
- ✓ Premise: The subject or result you are persuading the audience to embrace.
- ✓ *Points of Wisdom*: Your key talking points that reinforce your premise.
- ✓ Transitions: How you seamlessly transition from one idea to the next.
- ✓ Review: Remind your audience of your *points of wisdom*, sub-points, and characters introduced through your stories.
- ✓ Q & A: Answer your audience's questions.
- ✓ Call to Action: Challenge your audience to act on what they have learned.
- ✓ Strong Closing: Final story, thought, or quote that leaves your audience wanting more.

For more formal presentations, you have an introduction. This is what is said about your background and why you were selected to speak. In some circumstances, especially in Canada and the United Kingdom, you have an outro. This may be a review of your key ideas and the meaning it has to the emcee.

For professional speakers, the emcee may invite you back for more applause or discuss your book that will be made available. They may thank you and then tell the audience to meet with you.

WHICH LEADS US TO THE FRIPP PRESENTATION MODEL.

If you look at the diagram of the Fripp Presentation Model, you will see a circle at the top and a circle at the bottom.

These represent the first thirty seconds to three minutes strong opening and the last thirty seconds to three minutes strong conclusion. It's essential to begin and immediately connect with the audience and close on a high point. You may not necessarily write the presentation's opening first; however, you need to be aware of its importance. The purpose of your presentation opening is to arouse interest in the subject.

We compare the importance of the opening of your presentation to the opening scene of a movie, which gives us the *flavor* of the movie: comedy, drama, romance, thriller, or horror. We want your audience to elbow each other and say, "Wow, this is going to be good." Or, "What an interesting approach." Or at least, "This is *better* than I expected."

As you put together your remarks, ask yourself:

- "What do I know about this audience?"
- "What is the purpose of this presentation?"

The FRIPP Speech Model

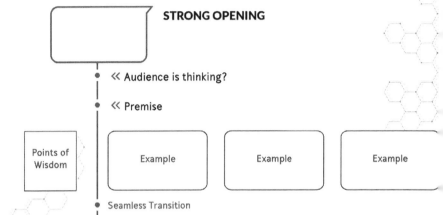

STRONG OPENING

- « Audience is thinking?
- « Premise

| Points of Wisdom | Example | Example | Example |

Seamless Transition

| Points of Wisdom | Example | Example | Example |

Seamless Transition

| Points of Wisdom | Example | Example | Example |

- « Review

« Answer Questions

STRONG CIOSING

- "Based on the title or event, what is this audience expecting?"
- "Are they interested in my subject, or do I have to persuade them of the importance?"
- "Why am I the best person to address the subject?"
- "How does my presentation fit into the overall meeting or event?"

You need to be aware of *who* you are addressing. Are there different segments of the audience, such as different disciplines or a variety of tiers within the same organization? If so, you need to make sure *they know you know* they are there.

After your opening, introduce your premise, the importance of this subject, or the result of acting on your advice.

You have plenty of options to transition into your premise, central theme, or subject (use whatever phrase makes the most sense to you).

You could say, "Welcome to how you can create an unforgettable presentation."

Or, "My premise is every ambitious professional can deliver unforgettable presentations."

Or, "Thank you for the invitation to help you increase sales with unforgettable sales presentations."

Or tie your message to the conference or meeting theme, "Your connection to the future is through unforgettable presentations."

Once you have decided what content will be included in your speech and focused on your premise, you are ready to organize your content into a strong structure.

Your talking points *prove your premise*. In other words, what steps will lead to your premise promise?

Your content and discussions are organized into chunks of content. Each chunk would stand alone as an eight-minute presentation.

Two of your authors are world champions of public speaking. To accomplish this, they had to prepare and deliver three separate presentations as the competition progressed. By the time the world championship was over, they and all the strong competitors who did well had developed the ability to create and polish content that has served them well. If there was a common theme, that theme could become a future keynote speech.

As you put your content into logical chunks based on your *points of wisdom*, here are some guidelines and options.

THE FIRST CHUNKING EXAMPLE: EXPLANATION, EXAMPLE, APPLICATION

Once you introduce your *point of wisdom*, add a needed explanation, an example of how your idea would apply, and then the application for this audience.

Example: *Point of wisdom*

"Our goal as presenters is to speak to be remembered and repeated. This often means going against what is commonly used by most people. For example, use time as a setup phrase."

ADD A NEEDED EXPLANATION

When you talk about a unit of time, as in "today," "in this seminar," or "our last fiscal year," your comments will be more memorable if you go against common practice and put them at the beginning of a sentence. If you are speaking to be remembered, the "setup phrase" is always at the beginning of your sentence to put what follows into context.

An example: If we were to turn on the news, you would hear a phrase put together traditionally, and it would sound like this: "Bill Gates delivered a speech on practical ways to eliminate disease at Yale University yesterday."

When you use the Fripp "time as a setup phrase" formula, it sounds like this: "Yesterday, at Yale University, Bill Gates delivered a speech on practical ways to eliminate disease."

FOLLOW THE MODEL OF WHEN, WHERE, WHO, AND WHAT HAPPENED.

What happened goes at the end of your statement. The setup phrase puts everything else into context. What Bill Gates discussed is more important to remember than yesterday or the day before, or Yale or Harvard.

THE APPLICATION

This goes against how your English teacher taught you to write. Try this in your emails and next few conversations, reports, or presentations. We promise you will have higher retention if you consistently practice this time as a setup technique.

How often have you heard, "You will be learning audience involvement techniques *today*" versus, "In the next four hours, you will be learning audience *involvement techniques*."

You see how we added time at the beginning and specifics: Four hours is the session length. Today is twenty-four hours.

THE SECOND CHUNKING EXAMPLE: PAST, PRESENT, FUTURE

You might take a historical view of your content.

For example, when our executive says, "Welcome to a brand-new company," it is logical to go back to its foundation and major turning points that led us to take the boldest move ever.

You can organize your content in this order.

WHAT WAS OUR GOAL IN THE PAST?

Based on experience, changes, and innovations:

Where are we now in the present?

How do we plan our future?

MOST YEARLY SALES MEETINGS USE THIS FORMULA.

"Welcome to the January sales conference.

As you reflect on our rich three-year sales results—congratulations! Your efforts are paying off.

Last year you produced five times more sales than we predicted.

It is appropriate to celebrate your success. However, after our celebrations, we cannot allow ourselves to become complacent.

The sales goals for this year are…"

Are you getting the hang of this?

THE THIRD CHUNKING EXAMPLE: DIFFERENT DEMOGRAPHICS

It would not be unusual for you to have an audience mixed of various disciplines, divisions of a company, or professionals from different companies or industries. At many of our speaking schools and coaching camps, the audience is made up of professional speakers or those who wish to be, business professionals, and sales professionals—the same balance of readers of our books.

In that case, you need to make sure that the content of your talking points includes how they relate to your subject. For example, from the point of view of payroll, HR, and IT.

HERE IS AN EXAMPLE

"As we introduce our new payroll system, you can feel confident that it will make your workload easier.

For our payroll professionals, you will spend less time answering our employees' frequent questions.

For our friends in HR, you will be able to stay more compliant with less time invested.

For our IT heroes, thank you for your work on this project. As you worked long hours to make this happen on time and under budget, you will all receive two extra vacation days with pay. Let us all congratulate them!"

ANOTHER CORPORATE EXAMPLE OF A "MIXED AUDIENCE" OF LOCAL, NATIONAL, AND INTERNATIONAL RESELLERS.

"As we introduce our new product line…

We have taken into consideration the economic environment in each of your areas.

For our local resellers, we have developed a marketing strategy that…

For our national resellers, we researched the differences in each state and…

For our international resellers, until now a smaller percentage of our market share, you will be excited to know we have doubled your marketing budget and hired a seasoned marketing agency in each of your countries."

HERE IS A PERSONAL STORY EXAMPLE THAT COULD BE PART OF THE LOCAL, REGIONAL, INTERNATIONAL CHUNK.

"When my father first opened our business, he sold to his friends and neighbors in the same town. He was excited at the progress, and his family did not need for anything.

My brother and I grew up knowing we would take over the business. Twenty years ago, when Dad finally took my mother on the world cruise he had promised her for thirty years, I became president.

Within three years, because of the internet, we expanded the business nationally. Ten years later, my daughter graduated from Stanford with a business degree and a fluency in Spanish and French.

As a university exchange student, my nephew studied in Japan. He left fluent in Japanese. If my dad were here, he would tell you, 'Yes, entrepreneurs, you can expand internationally. How? By raising smart children who have even smarter children.'

Thank you for the opportunity to tell *how* we built our business, *what* we have learned, and *why* it will be easier for you. Let us roll up our sleeves and get to work."

Remember to connect with your audience; it is important to make sure every audience segment is recognized.

THE FOURTH CHUNKING EXAMPLE: A STORY-FILLED KEYNOTE PRESENTATION

Within your content chunks, you will be using stories as examples.

> "A strong presentation structure gives you freedom to be creative."
>
> PATRICIA FRIPP

You may have all chunks of content made up of three stories: your personal experience, your audience's industry, and their company.

The first is what professional speakers call a "signature" story. This is from their own experience, is the classic favorite that always works with any audience, and introduces your first idea (*point of wisdom*) in each chunk of content.

The next story proves how this idea/suggestion works in the industry of the audience. The third story is specifically about the company you are speaking to. Perhaps you became a customer, were a mystery shopper, or interviewed their best associates.

This leads up to the close of your unforgettable presentation. This will be developed in a later chapter.

COMMON MISTAKES AT THIS STEP

Mistake #1: Not having a clear structure.

Mistake #2: Adding too much content.

Mistake #3: Creating your presentation in PowerPoint.

STEP #3 ACTIVITY

Build your structure around your premise. This step speeds up your process.

STEP #4

Create Your Strong Opening

"The purpose of the opening is to arouse interest in the subject."
Patricia Fripp

BEGIN WITH A strong opening that will arouse interest. At the beginning of a speech, presentation, seminar, client meeting, report to senior management, sales presentation, or any manner of presentation you deliver, you need to arouse interest in the subject. After all, we stand in the rain to see a movie. Would you stand in the rain to listen to your presentation?

You have thirty seconds to immediately command the attention of your audience. Don't waste it.

Certain speech openings captivate, mystify, and create an emotional bond that keeps an audience in the palm of the speaker's hand. What would you give to learn those essential opening words and techniques? What are great ways to bond instantly with an audience so you never see them dozing off, wandering out of the room, or turning off their webcam and focusing elsewhere?

Before we get to the sure-fire ways to begin for anyone who speaks in front of a group or would like to, let's discuss what you do not want to say or do. Don't be boring. Being too predictable is boring. Do not say, "Good morning, my name is John Smith, and I am going to talk about…"

In most circumstances, the audience knows who you are, and if you do introduce yourself, say something of interest first. If you are going to thank the introducer, you may want to just mouth "thank you" as you walk to the front of the room or verbalize your "thank you" after delivering an opening statement.

In their need to connect to the audience, speakers may open this way. "Good morning. It's so great to be here. The weather in your city is so much nicer than in mine. My husband came with me, and we are turning this into a mini-vacation." Nobody cares. They do not want a weather report on their city and may resent that you are taking advantage of this opportunity to serve them.

There are dozens of ways to open your presentation, and these techniques are not presented in any preferred order. The best way to begin depends on your style and the purpose of your message.

YOUR STRONG OPENING

You have now mined your life for brilliant content. You have your story file full of life experiences. You appreciate the value of crafting a simple structure based on a premise. Now, we are ready to consider your many options for your first thirty seconds. This chapter will focus on a few opening lines and opening techniques.

The common wisdom is to *get the audience's attention.* Mark goes deeper. The purpose of your opening is twofold: to get the audience's attention and to make an indelible connection. Ideally, a strong opening establishes a link to your audience and your subject.

We realize your career may require many types of presentations, from informal to formal, and for a handful of colleagues to a large audience on stage.

We are providing opening lines for both internal meetings and keynote speeches.

A bonus: In our coaching camps, we often use these opening lines to trigger ideas. If you say these out loud, what thoughts come to mind for stories? Capture any ideas and continue to build your story file.

Get To The Point Quickly

For internal meetings, your opening line might be any of the following:

- The purpose of this meeting is to…

- Thank you for the opportunity to…
- You will remember at our last meeting…
- Thank you for your support…
- We have an amazing opportunity to…
- There will never be a perfect time to…
- Congratulations…
- To put my report into historical perspective…
- Let us begin our meeting with a success story…
- We have an awesome responsibility…

These lines serve not only as a solid opening but can also be used as transition lines after a story or between speakers.

When your contribution is a segment as part of a team presentation, transition/opening lines are invaluable and add to the professionalism of the speakers.

The *get to the point* approach is best if you are reporting to your senior management.

"Good morning. On behalf of the dedicated four-person marketing team, thank you for the opportunity to present our third-quarter results and recommendations."

Or, "The recommendation of the entire team at Pacific Investments is to hire our recommended speech coach Mark Brown to help design your investor presentations. You can leave the rest of the planning and production to us."

SPEECH AND PRESENTATION
OPENING TECHNIQUES

Transport The Audience To A Different Time And Place

As you can tell, these lines launch into a story. The principle comes from our colleague story consultant Michael Hauge, who says, "Get into the scene late." Here are examples:

1. I wish you could have been there…

2. I'll never forget the first/last/only time I…

3. It was one of the most exciting days of my life…

4. It was the scariest moment of my life…

5. It was not exactly what I expected…

6. Come back with me…

7. Imagine…

8. When I was growing up, my father/mother/ teacher always said…

When you transport the audience to a scene, please be confident they want to find themselves there.

Connect To The Meeting Theme

1. I love your theme because…

2. What would the world be like without… (payroll professionals? first responders? engineers?)

3. Remember when… (The company or association was founded)

4. What a privilege to be part of a program focusing on "technology as tools to transport us into the future."

Convention committees invest months coming up with a theme for their conferences. Nothing delights them more than speakers incorporating the theme into their presentations.

Moderate A Meeting Or Conference

1. Welcome to… (the theme of the conference)

2. Congratulations… (you are part of the largest conference ever)

3. Sitting next to you are attendees from as close as and as far as…

4. They have been with our company from one week to forty-five years.

Let us repeat a point for emphasis. As you read earlier, being too predictable can be boring. We prefer the above to: "Good morning, ladies and gentlemen, we are so glad you are here," which is polite yet predictable.

OPENING TECHNIQUES

Whatever opening you choose, make sure it transitions into your premise. Here are some possibilities:

A Story

This is always an audience pleaser.

If you are speaking at a sales meeting:

A story of a sales professional or team showing dogged determination to close a sale.

If you have a client appreciation meeting:

A story of one of your clients thrilled to have a problem solved with your product, service, or advice.

If you are welcoming new associates to your team or company:

A story of when you first joined the company.

If you are discussing corporate finance:

A story of how changing one approach or making one simple change saved the company an incredible amount of money.

If you are introducing yourself to a new team:

A story of why you admire them or their results that led to your decision.

If you are introducing a new product:

Paint the picture of the client's life and business with this new product or feature.

If you are delivering an inspiring speech:

A story of overcoming a challenge or adversity or of a situation where a mentor showed you the way.

Interesting Statistics Or Little-Known Facts

If possible, start with an interesting statistic or little-known fact. No doubt you have several within your presentation. Bring one into the opening and add an emotion before it, "Would it interest/surprise/amaze you to know…"

"If you are a woman born after 1960, you will probably have more husbands than children. However, in all circumstances, we need to plan for our sound financial future…"

Patricia addressed 350 Seventh-Day Adventist pastors on "How to Design and Deliver a More Charismatic Sermon." A great way to build your credibility is to use a statistic from their world.

Her opening was, "Four-hundred sixty-five times in the Bible, it says: 'It came to pass.' It does not say it came to stay. Unless your sermon is well constructed, artfully crafted, and charismatically delivered, it will not come to stay in the hearts, minds, and lives of your congregation."

A Powerful Quotation

We recommend you use quotes from influencers in your own life, such as your parents, coach, or first boss. You never want to flavor the opening with the idea, "I have heard this before; nothing in this talk is likely to be new." Better-known quotes can be included later in your presentation.

A Question

If you ask a question such as, "Have you ever stood up to speak and forgotten what you wanted to say?" the most likely answer would be nods from the audience. The next time you ask this type of question, change it to "How often have you...?" The assumption is more than once, it will happen again, and your message becomes more urgent.

A Rhetorical Question

This is asked for effect, with no answer expected. "If I were to ask you..." Be aware of the possibility that someone will answer. Be ready to respond and move on. Mark spoke to youth audiences for twenty years and cautions against this technique with teenagers.

If you want to begin by asking a question, forget clichés such as: "Who wants to make more money?" An opening question must be more profound, more intriguing, even a question that doesn't necessarily have an answer.

"How are you going to change your marketing strategy now that you have identified thirteen strong competitors instead of the three you faced a few years ago?"

A Challenge

A challenge is expected after your presentation. You may also want to challenge your audience to take action, give them information to be in a position to take action, and restate your challenge near the end.

Tie To The Headlines

News headlines are a simple way to make your prepared presentation appear to be spontaneous. Hold that day's *Wall Street Journal* and ask, "Did you have time to read the *Wall Street Journal* this morning? The headline on page three ties directly to my presentation." Connect the headline to your subject, and your instant customization helps you look brilliant and your topic relevant.

Bold Claim Or Big Promise

A bold claim could be, "In the next two hours, you will learn more about presentation skills than in your four years at college." Of course, if you make a bold claim, you must be able to meet that claim and exceed the audience's expectations.

Find Immediate Connection To The Audience (So What? Me Too)

The late Jim Rohn was a magnificent motivational speaker. When Patricia was touring with him in Australia, he gave her this advice: "When you're introduced, you are given a wonderful introduction, and the audience is thinking, *So what?* What you want them to think is, *Me too.*"

Find common ground. If you have a relationship with the company, have the introducer introduce you as one of the customers. For example, AAA Insurance introduced Patricia by her policy number, and United Airlines introduced her by her frequent flyer number. When Darren spoke at

Wells Fargo, his introducer said, "And here to present a customer's point of view is account number _____." It's fun. More importantly, it connects. All professionals are endeared to people who do business with them. You can then open with, "I'm not here as a presenter. I'm here as one of your loyal customers."

Read A Letter, Email, Or Review

Whenever you receive a complimentary letter, email, or magazine article, no doubt you want to ask yourself, "Is there a way I could use this in the opening of a presentation?" Or perhaps, consider the opposite. The legendary guitarist, and Patricia's brother, Robert Fripp, is also an interesting and articulate speaker. He begins many of his presentations reading a bad review of his work. He then critiques the review and debunks the credibility of the critic. This creates empathy and laughter from the audience.

Compliment The Audience

Find something praiseworthy about your audience and deliver it with sincerity. Patricia helped a marketing executive to create this opening: "What a magnificent opportunity to present the marketing tool kit to the best sales team in the pharmaceutical industry. You spoke, we listened, and we are about to unveil the results of your request."

Relevant Humor

A joke is risky because of the high probability that your audience has heard it before, even if it's funny. We recommend that you uncover humor in a real-life story and make it funnier with exaggeration. At the meeting, you may see, hear, or experience a funny situation that everyone is aware of. In that case, go with your prepared opening, then slip in the humorous situation. Unless you are experienced, it is not a good idea to begin with an untested line.

COMMON MISTAKES AT THIS STEP

Mistake #1: Not having a prepared opening and just winging it.

Mistake #2: Having an opening that's irrelevant to your premise.

Mistake #3: Beginning with your premise.

Mistake #4: Opening with small talk and blah, blah, blah.

Mistake #5: Starting with "I want to talk about…"

Mistake #6: Introducing yourself after being introduced.

STEP #4 ACTIVITY

Write your strong opening. You have plenty of choices. However, choose one that will smoothly transition into your premise. Why not come up with three options and test them with trusted friends?

STEP #5

Create Your Compelling Close

"Your last words linger."
Patricia Fripp

LOSE TO REINFORCE your premise and inspire action.

Every great singer opens with their second-best song and closes with their best.

In a perfect world, your close would be the highlight of your speech. Then you look out and see your audience leap to their feet, applauding. Bill Gove, the first president of the National Speakers Association, said, "A standing ovation says more about the audience than the speaker." In other words, a mediocre speech can get that result from a direct sales organization. Whereas the best crafted and delivered presentation given to enthusiastic actuaries may not.

However, you can rely on a surefire formula to close your presentation.

OUR SIX-STEP FORMULA TO CAPTIVATE YOUR AUDIENCE AT THE END OF YOUR PRESENTATION

1. A rhetorical question.

Ask your audience a rhetorical question based on your premise. For example, "How do you perfect your presentation skills?" This helps the audience focus on the premise of your presentation.

"How can you double your sales with your existing database?"

"How can you as a leader inspire action and commitment in your team?"

"How can a payroll manager sell themselves and their ideas to the upper management?"

"How can you make this year your *best* year?"

Now your audience is refocused on your premise.

2. Review your *points of wisdom*.

As you revisit your talking points, tie them into your examples. We recommend you build rehearsal into your everyday life. For example, "Would rehearsing on the treadmill work for you?"

"Record your presentations and review them as if you were looking at another speaker. What would you tell that speaker they are doing well? What would you encourage them to do to improve?"

"As a sales professional, beware of data decay. Review the bounced emails when you send out your monthly customer updates."

"Remember Roger? After he implemented the four strategies you have been introduced to, he became the top realtor in his city. They are 1, 2, 3, 4…"

3. Challenge your audience.

Remind the audience about the benefits of taking your advice and why your information is relevant to their concerns. You may want to say, "Thank you for your active participation and enthusiasm for our subject. I challenge you to take your notes and reread them while you can still read your handwriting!"

"I recommend you teach one of your friends or colleagues what you have learned. Teaching someone else is the best way to reinforce the ideas. Create an action plan, and prioritize what you want to implement first."

"For a prize, who would like to announce what is the first action they will take to implement the new sales plan?"

Yes, rewarding participation is a good practice. The best leadership lesson works in presentations. Performance that is rewarded tends to be repeated.

Yes, we recommend you use the word "challenge," as this builds on the naturally competitive nature of most humans.

4. Call to action.

This ties into the challenge. Make sure you give specific next steps to help your audience implement what they have learned. Invite them to make a decision, and act right now.

5. Q & A

After your review, most likely your audience will have questions.

As with an in-person presentation, always review your key ideas with a virtual audience before concluding. Then ask, "Before my closing remarks, what questions do you have?"

If you plan to include Q & A, indicate how much time has been allotted. To keep the session flowing, Patricia recommends you say, "What are your short, specific questions?" Be sure to let your audience know when you will take two final questions. With virtual presentations, after each *point of wisdom*, before you transition to the next chunk of content, why not add a slide with a question mark? This reminds you of your flow, and it gives the audience time to engage. Upfront, ask the introducer or moderator to tell the audience you will be doing this.

If you are your moderator, let the audience know to add their questions when they have them. Our advice is if you have an audience of more than a handful, have a moderator. Not all questions need to be answered if they are off-topic. Or, if three attendees ask the same question, they can be combined. A moderator has more time to evaluate the questions than you, the speaker. It is a good idea to have a couple of on-point questions prepared in case none are asked.

If you speak on a complex subject, it is best to answer questions throughout your presentation. With longer sessions, half-day, full-day, or multiple-day training, have interaction throughout your session, not only to answer questions, but also to change the experience to keep everyone engaged.

If you do not have time for Q & A, you may want to include, "As we do not have time for Q & A, let me answer my three most frequently asked questions. They are…"

Patricia works with many engineers who speak at their company's customer conferences, where the rule is to allow ten minutes for Q & A. Many of their audience members are not comfortable asking questions. She prepares them the same way.

"No doubt you want to know…" or, "At this point, we usually are asked…" Also, as there are usually two presenters per session, she has them prepare questions for each other in case the audience has no questions.

Henry Kissinger once said at a press conference, "Does anyone have any questions for my answers?" He meant he would hold onto his agenda no matter where the press tried to take him.

Ending a presentation ineffectively can undermine your message. Wrapping up your talk with a Q & A session may seem like a natural choice; however, this can be a mistake. If you end with a Q & A, you risk a lone, ill-humored audience member stating a negative opinion—rather than asking a relevant question—diluting the message you intended to leave with your audience. Even if you receive excellent questions during a Q & A, remember that you still must conclude your presentation by delivering a closing as powerful as the opening.

6. End On A High Point: Options For Closing Techniques.

The last thirty seconds of your speech must send your audience out energized and fulfilled. This means you need to finish your talk with something inspirational that supports your theme.

The Circular Technique. As a discipline, it's wise to always revisit your opening, whether you use this or not. In the *circular technique*, the opening and closing generate the same emotion or have corresponding circumstances or situations. For example, Patricia opened her keynote to the American Cemetery Association with the story of her experience when her mother died. Using the circular technique, she led into her close with: "At the beginning of my presentation you heard my experience when my mother died. Let me close with my brother's experience that he wrote in the liner notes of his CD *Blessing of Angels*. 'Life is what we are given; living is what we do with it.'"

The opening showed her perspective, and the closing gave her brother Robert's perspective.

In the 1990s, Mike Powell was a senior scientist at Genentech working on developing an AIDS vaccine. Patricia helped him get ready to speak to her professional women's organization. She suggested, "We do not spend time with scientists; tell us what it is like."

Mike opened with, "Being a scientist is like doing a jigsaw puzzle…in a snowstorm…at night…when you don't have all the pieces, and you don't have the picture you are trying to create."

Everyone sat forward.

He closed by saying, "At the beginning of my presentation, you heard about the frustrations of being a scientist, so many ask, 'Why would you want to do that?'" Mike told them about a particularly information-intensive medical conference he had attended.

The final speaker walked from the back of the room to the lectern and said, "I am a thirty-two-year-old wife and mother of two. I have AIDS. Please work fast."

Everyone jumped to their feet, applauding.

Mike received a standing ovation for his first speech to a lay audience. His presentation was successful because he had simplified the complexity of his job and made it a human-interest story, both from his point of view and from that of the patients they were dedicated to helping.

The Story Close. A story is always a good way to close a presentation. Be sure that it reinforces your premise and drives your message home.

The End-Of-The-Story Close. This closing technique involves a story told early in the speech, maybe even in the opening. As far as the audience is concerned, the story had a successful conclusion. In the closing, you reveal one more detail about the story, in effect, revealing the next and concluding scene of the story.

Here's an example from Hall of Fame speaker Tony Alessandra's presentation on customer service. He opened with a story about a frustrating experience dealing with calling an airline for the second time, only to find the cost of his ticket was now six hundred dollars more than thirty minutes before. He heard, "Sir, there is nothing I can do for you. The only suggestion is you could call the president of the airline." Case closed. This was a satisfying conclusion to the story. Forty-five minutes later, after his review, challenge, call to action, and Q & A, the audience loved his message. He then took two steps forward and said, "So, I called the president of the airline and said…" Everybody laughed because by now, their mind was no longer on the opening. This was an effective use of the end-of-the-story close.

A Perspective-Changing Close. This closing prompts the audience to think differently about a situation, others, or themselves.

Mark uses this technique in his presentation "Stronger Together" to discuss various roles and responsibilities within an organization. During the presentation, he acknowledges that some positions may feel minor and almost insignificant and emphasizes why they're important. He closes with, "Your role may seem insignificant, but *you* are invaluable. Know your role, play your part, and you will all be *stronger together.*" Used effectively, this technique will prompt your audience to change their perspective.

Sometimes, by their response, your audience will tell you that you have made a perspective-changing statement. Darren experienced that when delivering his "Path to Powerful Presentations." He noticed every time he made a certain statement, the audience instantly wrote it down. His audience was telling him that he had a "perspective-changing statement." He realized the statement would be significantly more powerful at the end of his presentation as a perspective-changing close, and he moved it to his conclusion.

The Emergency Close. As the name suggests, this is a close to have "in your back pocket," which means prepared and ready when needed. If you must unexpectedly end your presentation, it's important to still leave your message on a high point. When you have the confidence of being prepared, you can relax.

Mark delivered a youth program and was assured that he had a specific time window to deliver his presentation. With fifteen minutes to go, he saw an administrator at the back of the room waving frantically, showing him a five-minute signal. He quickly called on his emergency closing, which appeared seamless to his audience. Had he not been prepared, the ending would have been rushed and sloppy. The additional benefit? The client was happy. If you are a seasoned presenter, you know it is not a matter of *if*, but *when* it will happen again.

World Champion Ed Tate competed in the World Championship of Public Speaking, where speakers *must* adhere to strict time limits or face disqualification. His speech was so humorous that the audience's laughter used up more time than he had anticipated. He was forced to use his emergency close. Had he not done so, he would not be a World Champion of Public Speaking.

The Fripp Remember Me Close. This technique gives the audience a unique reason to remember you. Here's Patricia's example:

"Thank you for being an appreciative audience. I hope you will remember me. Fripp. However, much more important than remembering me, remember what Fripp stands for: Frequently Reinforce Ideas that are Productive and Profitable."

Invariably, audience members approached her afterward, saying, "What was that final line?" What are they doing? Writing down her name, which is wisely her website.

Last Words Linger: Bonus Close. The last line of your story may be powerful enough. Patricia recommends her sales and technical clients make this a habit. It reminds their prospect of one of their significant benefits, part of their value proposition, or major feature of their technology. As the sales professionals or systems engineers are about to leave the boardroom or client office or close the virtual product demo, almost as an after-thought, they say, "Remember, 99 percent of the Fortune-500 do business with us." Or,

"Remember, 157 profitable quarters." Or, "We are large enough to satisfy your needs, and small enough you will be a valued customer." What is the number one benefit you offer? When you close your presentations incorporating these six techniques and the bonus, you leave your audience wanting more.

COMMON MISTAKES AT THIS STEP

Mistake #1. Closing on questions.

Mistake #2. Not closing with your strongest point.

Mistake #3. Introducing a point you don't develop.

Mistake #4. No call to action.

STEP #5 ACTIVITY

Write your compelling close. If you wish, select three options, and test them. Ask a few trusted friends for their opinions, and decide which closing works best for you.

Make it Unforgettable!

"Your story is about you, yet it's for them."
Mark Brown

ERE IS HOW to be remembered and repeated. When you do this, you speak to the audience of your audience.

We guarantee if you've heard a good speech, sermon, or business presentation, that you enjoyed and remembered, at least one of the reasons that made it memorable was the stories.

Everybody loves a good story, and that is their power. No matter our culture, we grow up feeling that being told a story is somehow a reward. Stories are how we learn values and our family's legacy. When we're in school, stories make history come alive. In business, we quickly discover that stories help us explain complex issues and are the best way to connect to coworkers, customers, and audiences of all sizes.

Wise leaders, sales professionals, and speakers do well to develop an arsenal of great stories that provide clear, dramatic examples. Good stories help differentiate us from our competition.

Good stories that are interesting, memorable, and illustrate your message can inspire and motivate, train and teach, convince and persuade.

When an audience of one or one thousand listens to your stories, they must find them interesting, have an emotional connection to them, and find the lesson to be learned. It must be obvious how the story ties to the point you are making at that time in your presentation.

Your audience does not remember everything that they hear. With a well-told story, they *see* it happening. This increases the likelihood of your presentation being remembered and repeated.

Our friend and Hollywood script consultant Michael Hague teaches, "The purpose of a story is to elicit emotion."

When Darren spoke in Taiwan, his meeting planner Teresa said, "You were here six years ago, and I will never forget your story of how nervous you were your first time on stage." She then demonstrated a gesture that Darren uses every time he tells it. The emotion of the story resonated with her, and she remembered it six years later. That is being remembered and repeated.

UNFORGETTABLE STORIES

Many speakers mistakenly think that for a story to be unforgettable, it must be dramatic and life-changing. In reality, people relate to simple stories from everyday life to which we can attribute meaning where there usually is none. Darren's early mentor Dave Fitzgerald told him, "Stop trying to find the story that will launch your career, and instead take the stories you have and perfect them."

Since then, Darren has created a story model.

DARREN'S THEN/NOW STORY MODEL

Now let's look at the components to create unforgettable stories. Stories are about people and change. We see the situation through the eyes of a person. That may or may not be you. The first step is to introduce a *relatable character.*

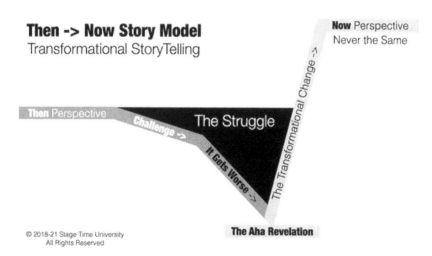

Then -> Now Story Model
Transformational StoryTelling

Now Perspective
Never the Same

Then Perspective

Challenge ->

The Struggle

It Gets Worse ->

The Transformational Change ->

The Aha Revelation

For that, we need their backstory: enough information for your audience to see the character, identify with them, relate to their emotion or situation, and empathize with them. A good way to do that is from "a day in their life."

This is the "before" picture. Adding dialogue will help your audience understand and relate to the situation.

Struggle: A challenge is the hook to any good story. It could be self-induced or from an outside source. This is called the inciting incident in a movie—the moment from which there is no turning back. The audience wants to know what happens. Increase the conflict and tension. The result of this is? Can the stakes get raised? Who else could the conflict affect? How can the situation get worse? Can your audience feel and/or relate to the struggle?

Revelation: The "aha" or the transformational lesson learned. What changed or dramatically transformed the situation or the character? This may be self-realization or advice delivered from a guru in the story.

"If there is no change of emotion in at least one character, there is no story."

DARREN LACROIX

Perspective: This is the "after" picture. How has your character or the situation dramatically changed? Use dialogue as self-talk or as a conversation with another character. As you can tell, dialogue drives your story forward. Your character should be transformed through the course of their journey through your story.

When properly applied, these components and techniques will enhance your presentation and help to make it unforgettable.

NOBODY CAN RESIST A GOOD STORY WELL TOLD

Patricia works with sales teams to use stories to increase sales. She asks them, "Have you noticed it often seems as if our prospects are trained to resist a sales presentation? Nobody can resist a good story when it is well told."

When you have strong competition, you must tell better stories than your competition. In this context, we tell stories that relate to how we improve our client's conditions. You may call them examples or case histories. They are stories. The stories will go into two categories. The first and most important are about your satisfied clients enjoying the benefits of your product or service.

The happy-client story formula is situation, solution, success. If I were to ask you, "Can I have a reference of one of your clients who has benefited from your service?" You would say, "Yes, Patricia, feel free to call Diane Brooks. Like you, she is a successful entrepreneur who needed our help to manage her business finances, accounting, and bookkeeping. We have worked with her for the last five years, and she is satisfied with our service."

Your sales stories must be true, just not 100 percent accurate as stories shrink time. You put what may have been multiple meetings and calls into one conversation.

To paraphrase the great movie director Alfred Hitchcock, "Movies are like life with all the dull parts left out."

This is the situation. Imagine when you first met your client and they said, "Help," and clearly articulated their problem.

"Help, our current technology partner costs us too much."

Or "Help, we are not compliant."

Or, "Help, we assumed experienced technology professionals would be able to effectively tell our story."

In good storytelling, the situation is always told in the client's words.

The client's situation is their problem, the pain is the same for the prospect you are now talking to.

The solution is what you did for the client with your product, service, or technology. This can be in your words. You explain your process so that your prospect can see what it is like to work with you. You can use phrases such as:

"What Diane benefited from is the usual three-step approach we take with each new client: First we…" This also answers your prospect's unasked question. "If we say yes, what happens next?"

The third part of this formula is the success. This is the end of the story, the happily ever after—how did you improve their condition?

Just as with the situation, this needs to be in the client's words. You can repeat their glowing comments. When you use their words, they will be more expansive than you would say about yourself. However, their words are specific.

Let us go back to our example about Diane.

"Patricia, if Diane were here, she would tell you, 'When I first talked to Jenna at Profit Results, my accounting was in a total mess. My last bookkeeper had dropped the ball, which resulted in $3,000 in fines and penalties. Even though the professionals at Profit Results had nothing to do with creating my problem, they went to bat for me. Within three weeks of hiring them, not only did I get my $3,000 refunded, but they also found me more legitimate write-offs that resulted in another $8,762 refund. In the first two months of hiring them, their efforts resulted in enough refunds to pay for their services for the next four years. They have my loyalty for life. You can't go wrong talking to Jenna.'"

You are using dialogue in your script when you add quotation marks. If you just report on the dialogue, you are not. For example, Diane told us how her last bookkeeper had dropped the ball and resulted in costly penalties.

> **"Don't sell, just tell a story."**
> DARREN LACROIX

YOUR FOUNDATIONAL PHRASE

Within many of your stories is a foundational phrase. This is a short sentence that gets your point across or summarizes your story. These phrases add clarity and help your audience become clear on your message. These phrases are both memorable and easy to remember.

Here are some of our favorite foundational phrases:

"Stage time, stage time, stage time." –Darren

"Skillset without mindset will leave your audience upset." –Darren

"Your story is about you, yet it's for them." –Mark

"Your audience wants to hear you, and they really want to know you." –Mark

"Life is a series of sales situations, and the answer is no if you don't ask." –Patricia

"Speak to be remembered and repeated." –Patricia

Your audience will be able to repeat your foundational phrase to their friends and associates.

YOUR RELATIONSHIP WITH YOUR AUDIENCE

We recommend two ways to connect to your audience: intellectually and emotionally. Logic makes you think; emotion makes you act. The intellectual connection will come from your content and the logic around how you make your case.

Emotional connection is easier. There are three ways that you can emotionally connect with your audience. First is through stories. Second, you-focused language or what we call the "I-You" ratio. Balance how often you say "I" compared to "you" or "we." Third is to speak more as an audience advocate and see your message from your audience's point of view. After all, everyone is more interested in themselves than you.

We suggest you remove the following from your presentations:

- "I am going to talk about…"
- "What I would like to talk about…"
- "What I am going to do first is…"

Instead, substitute, "Great news, you are about to learn ten techniques guaranteed to make your presentations unforgettable."

Make a list of you-focused phrases that would work in your presentations. Here are a few to begin:

- "In your experience…"
- "How often have you…"
- "You can feel confident…"
- "It might interest you to know…"
- "If I were to ask you…"

Patricia helped a sales executive from a major hotel with this short presentation to bring a convention to San Francisco. They had strong competition with two other cities. When the competition is tough, the best presentation wins. It was a $500,000 event. This was her recommended you-focused opening:

"In the next eight minutes… *You* will decide, the best decision *you* can make for *your* association and *your* members is to bring *your* convention to San Francisco and the Fairmont Hotel."

That is five *you* or *your*, and one Fairmont. That is a solid emotional connection.

Speak as an audience advocate. You want to be remembered as an intelligent and dynamic presenter. However, if an audience of any size feels you are concerned and interested in them, they will consider you unforgettable. Especially in the situation when your audience members have no choice but to be there. Your content is important. However, focus your content on the audience's point of view.

Personalize your message: Your premise statement helps. In preparation for your presentation, find out from the organizer why you? Interview company associates or members of the association. Ask how your major points relate to their company or industry and ask: "Can you give me a specific example?" Interview individuals who demonstrate activities or behavior that you recommend in your speech. You can read industry and company newsletters, corporate reports, and mission statements. Learn their buzz words, know their acronyms, and incorporate them into your presentation.

Then it becomes unforgettable. When Mark delivered a keynote presentation in Quebec, Canada, he told his opening story in French. Twenty years earlier, in high school, he had taken French and was not even remotely fluent. Even so, because of his effort, the audience jumped to their feet in a standing ovation *after his first four minutes.* In Taiwan, Patricia opened ten presentations in Chinese and delivered her foundational phrases in Chinese. Even though her interpreter had to translate her attempts at Chinese, the audience laughed and loved it. In both situations, the audiences appreciated the attempt to connect and the incredible effort to do their best to carry it off. They established a strong connection and gave their audiences an unforgettable experience. Please do not underestimate the value of hours of work and preparation.

Become a mystery shopper. Patricia became considered an industry expert in manufactured housing by taking a day in her life to visit eight different outlets and pretend to be a customer. She noted what each sales professional did well and when they overlooked a major opportunity.

Become a customer. As you read in an earlier chapter, you can be introduced by your account, policy, or frequent flyer number when you are already a customer. When Patricia was booked to speak for the Bartlett Tree company, she called and made an appointment for them to inspect her trees. Her opening story made two of their employees sound like the heroes they were for how they treated her. When they rebooked her, she interviewed four sales professionals and went on a sales call with one of them. Then, dressed in a

Bartlett t-shirt, hardhat, and work gloves, she went to work, sweeping up the tree cuttings and bagging and dragging them to the truck. Yes, she loved every minute of it.

Another way to become memorable and unforgettable. Dramatize your message and the audience's experience. Darren's friend Vince Antonucci is one of Las Vegas's most charismatic—and, as you will soon discover, creative— ministers. Most of his congregation will tell you his sermons are unforgettable. He is a prolific author and has a great sense of humor. He grew up with a Jewish mother and gambling-addict father who ended up on *America's Most Wanted*. He became a Christian in college by doing his best to prove the Bible was not true. He left a potentially lucrative career in law to become a pastor. By now, you know this is a colorful character.

Vince delivered a series of messages entitled "Tattooed." His premise was we all carry harmful baggage based on lies we still believe from our past.

Over several church services, a tattoo artist worked on a segment of Vince's tattoo while Vince was delivering his sermon. As you can imagine, this created so much curiosity that it attracted the media.

His audience kept growing because they wanted to see the finished tattoo, which Vince proudly revealed on the third week.

Vince had accepted the identity of *unloved* because his father had been abusive and, as you read, ended up on

America's Most Wanted. Although Vince has struggled to shed the unloved identity, his finished tattoo read, "The One Jesus Loves." His message and the experience were unforgettable.

When setting up the context of your illustration, clarity is critical. Just as stories are the heartbeat of a presentation, setting up your illustration is essential for success.

Grab a creative friend or co-worker and have a brainstorming session. Being creative in isolation is extremely difficult. Creativity works best over tea or in a dark smoky bar, making notes on a soggy cocktail napkin. Don't self-edit. Remember, crazy ideas often lead to the most brilliant concepts.

As you may remember, in an earlier life when it was a new industry, Patricia was San Francisco's number one men's hairstylist. Years later, her best client gave her the crazy idea she should "deliver a speech while cutting hair. Why not combine the career areas you excelled in?" That idea led to a stage set to look like a salon, three clients in chairs covered in drapes that said, "Don't Get Clipped; Get Fripped." The audience was greeted by attractive women welcoming them to the salon and asking, "Do you have an appointment?" Others on stage were buffing the client's shoes and filing their nails. Patricia's message included her razor-sharp wit and cutting-edge strategies.

COMMON MISTAKES AT THIS STEP

Mistake #1. Not being committed to doing the work.

Mistake #2. Not using you-focused language.

Mistake #3. Not making your stories transformational.

STEP #6 ACTIVITIES

Create your foundational phrase.

Adapt the story formulas to stories you are now telling.

Review your presentations for you-focused language.

Consider how you could have personalized past presentations.

Without getting a tattoo or cutting hair, how could you add drama?

Check out our video examples on:

www.DeliverUnforgettablePresentations.com/bonus

STEP #7

Own Your Stage

*"You must connect before you can
inform, inspire, or influence."*
Darren LaCroix

YOU MUST PREPARE like a pro for primetime.

By now, the excitement is building, and you are
ready to stand up, speak out, and feel as if you own
the stage.

Prolific humor author and Bob Hope's head comedy writer
Gene Perret said, "You need to know your material so well
your words fall flawlessly from your lips."

You have prepared your presentation, added your visual aids,
and rehearsed. Before you take the stage or turn on your
webcam, pause for a moment and focus your attention.

YOUR INTENTION MATTERS

Audiences have become jaded. They can sense inauthenticity in their leaders and speakers. They can tell if you are attempting to impress them with your knowledge and eloquence rather than serving them.

Mark admits that earlier in his career, he accepted a speaking engagement because he wanted to meet a celebrity who was on the program. Mark's presentation didn't go well, and he only had thirty seconds with him when the celebrity was hurrying to his car. Mark felt he had disappointed himself, the audience, and the event planner. He committed never to make that mistake again.

Years later, before Darren competed against eight of the best presenters in the world, Mark could see his ego creeping in. He reminded Darren: "Tomorrow morning, you have the privilege to influence two thousand lives. What will you do with that opportunity? Focus on them, not yourself."

In 2019, when Mark and Darren launched their Unforgettable Presentations podcast, they intended to serve the listeners first. They knew that if they served first, clients would follow. Fewer than two years later, their podcast was ranked in the top 1.5 percent of 2.5 million podcasts globally. Intention and content that served their target audience led to the success.

PREPARE FOR PRIMETIME

Presentation preparation is the difference between good, great, and unforgettable. When Darren was facing the most important presentation of his career, he received this powerful advice from coach David Brooks: "Let no one out-prepare you." He took David's words to heart, and history was made. That presentation, on that day, to that audience, changed the course of Darren's career and business.

There are times we realize a presentation is going to change our future. Often, we discover it has. Our preparation and our intention go hand in hand. Robert Fripp, brother of Patricia Fripp, has played guitar for over fifty years. *Rolling Stone* magazine named him the forty-second best guitarist in the world.

His band, King Crimson, is legendary. Every day, on tour or at home, Robert practices to keep the muscle memory in his hands and to stay at the top of his profession. He explains, "Every time you step on stage, 'it is the assumption of innocence within a context of experience.' Yes, I have played the music before; however, each time my foot steps on stage, it is for the first time. For this audience, in this theatre, on this day."

TO SCRIPT OR NOT TO SCRIPT?

The Fripp Presentation Model is your roadmap to give you confidence that you have your content organized logically. The next question is to script or not to script?

That depends on what works with you, your style, and the potential impact of your presentation. Patricia helps most of her clients develop a script. Technical and leadership presentations that will be shared thousands of times on YouTube and the company's website need to be on target and on message.

As she explains to some of her sales team clients, "You have sixty minutes to win a ten-million-dollar piece of business. Every word counts." Patricia claims, "My work is done when a sales team will debate for ten minutes on the choice of one word."

Few people can write conversationally. The written word is for the eye; the spoken word is for the rhythm. You must deliver your presentation out loud. Sentences that are too long are difficult to say. Patricia says, "I ask my clients questions, pull the words out of their mouths, polish them up, pop them back in, and say, 'Write that down.'"

We recommend, and insist with our clients, that you have your presentation structure, and hold the overview in your mind. Then script your opening, call to action, and closing, word for word. The best way to get your complete script is to deliver your presentation. If you need an audience, invite a few friends. Record your presentation and have it transcribed. Many fast and inexpensive transcription services are available. Now you have a conversational, spoken script. Next, edit, tighten, improve the quality of your word choice, and internalize your new, conversational-sounding speech.

MEMORIZE OR INTERNALIZE: WHAT IS THE DIFFERENCE?

We say, "Know it so well you can forget it." This is the muscle memory Robert Fripp mentioned. If your spouse elbowed you in the middle of the night, could you deliver your speech?

To do this, build rehearsal into your everyday life. Practice one story at a time with family and friends. You could rehearse as you walk. Patricia prefers to rehearse on a treadmill. As both sides of your body move, your left brain keeps your structure, and your right brain helps create wonderful phrases, not in your script.

Why not record your script and talk along with your own words? Mark often listens to recordings while riding on his lawnmower. Use whatever process works best for you.

REHEARSAL IS THE WORK

Sir Michael Caine says, "Rehearsal is the work; performance is the relaxation."

You can rehearse alone, and for important presentations rehearse with your colleagues or friends. Rehearse as you will deliver. Dress and speak as you will for the presentation.

When you begin your presentation, stand still with your feet shoulder-width apart. Patricia says, "How you stand as you open represents the stability of your ideas and the stability of your organization." While the audience is getting used to your voice, don't distract them with unnecessary movement.

Certainly, you do not need to stand still for the whole speech. If you wish to, fine. There will be movement from your gestures and facial expressions.

When you move, move on purpose, and continue to make eye contact with your audience. Move as you transition from one segment to the next. Move on a movement-specific phrase, "As I walked into the boss's office."

Each time you rehearse your presentation, record and review.

There are three versions of every presentation you deliver: the one you created, the one you delivered, and the next one you will deliver based on your experience and review.

MASTER YOUR SPEAKING AREA

Your goal is to have a confident command of your stage. As part of his rehearsal, Darren strategically places index cards containing his *points of wisdom* on different areas of the floor. These match the structure and flow of his presentation. The key is finding what techniques work for you and practicing them consistently.

Remember: when presenting, never wander or pace back-and-forth like a caged lion. Move with purpose and stand still when delivering key lines or dialogue and your *points of wisdom*.

REHEARSE WITH A TRIAL AUDIENCE

Once you have internalized your message and rehearsed your presentation, find a trial audience. Your delivery will change when you have faces in front of you that react.

If you speak at your company meeting representing your department, your colleagues have a vested interest in your success.

Patricia advises her clients who deliver presentations to win large pieces of business to take a week before the big day to rehearse. Each morning, deliver the presentation for different teams in the company. Get them to ask the toughest questions, record the sessions, and review. Analyze the feedback and how well the tough questions were answered. Together, debate the best way to handle them. Repeat the process every day with another group.

DEPENDING ON YOUR SITUATION

Your trial audience can comprise your co-workers, fellow Toastmasters, mastermind colleagues, and friends. If your primetime presentation is delivered virtually, then get a virtual audience.

Whoever you pick, make sure they have your best interest at heart. It is helpful if they are knowledgeable about public speaking. Everyone can tell you how they felt. However, the closer to the demographics of your actual audience, the better. You want specific feedback. Not just "That was great."

Take note of the comments that are frequently mentioned. In rehearsal, look for smiles, nods, and notetaking, which indicate that you are connecting with your audience.

GET A COACH

Executives have coaches because many of their direct reports can't or won't give them feedback. Getting a professional coach is one of the fastest ways to improve and shorten your learning curve.

For nine years, Darren struggled to improve until Mark dramatically changed the trajectory of his skills. Patricia was already a Hall of Fame speaker before she hired her first coach. Being good does not mean you can't become great.

BEFORE RAPPORT

Your relationship with your audience, organizer, and client is best established long before you set foot on stage. Darren calls this "before rapport." This varies depending on your situation.

If you speak at a customer user conference, use social media to promote the event and your session. Let your customers know you will be looking for them.

If you are training for your company, connect with your trainees in advance. Perhaps send them a video message, and let them know what they can look forward to when virtual. When live, shake hands and introduce them to each other.

Professional speakers can make videos to help promote events, along with social media, articles for their publications, and pre-event surveys. Most importantly, meet all deadlines.

When presenting virtually, always schedule a "tech check" and rehearsal before the day of the event. This is particularly helpful if you are unfamiliar with their online platform.

MORE BEFORE RAPPORT

Meet with your event planner and/or client and the A/V tech team. Conduct a complete tech check, and walk the stage, noting any spots that creak or squeak. Familiarize yourself with the room, identify and correct any potential distractions. Review the meeting agenda with your event planner or client and confirm that there are no new changes. Then get a good night's rest.

Meet with your introducer. Confirm they have your introduction and not your bio, which is considerably longer. Although you would have sent it in advance, have a copy with you. Confirm they realize this is written to set the right tone and segue into your presentation.

Your introduction is designed to tell your audience why you are the right speaker on this topic and give your credentials. We highly recommend you sell the importance of the subject to the audience before your credentials. Do not leave this important step to anyone else.

When you have a connection to your audience, your introduction can tell your credentials and then, "That is not why we invited her. We invited Mary because when she was a sales manager in our industry, she helped drive the largest sales in our industry's history." Or, "Our speaker is an award-winning speaker and bestselling author. That is not why we hired him. We hired John because he is one of our loyal clients. Welcome account number…"

Recently, video introductions have become quite popular because they can be more informative, engaging, and entertaining than a traditional introduction. If you opt for a video introduction, make sure it's professionally created, short and tight, and has an emotional connection.

BEFORE RAPPORT RITUAL

Some speakers do not want to be seen by their audience before they walk on stage. Patricia's instinct is always to wander around and enjoy short, friendly conversations with attendees before the program begins. Mark often speaks to attendees in the hallway and the room before his presentation. Darren meets and greets at the door as attendees walk in. These are simple and effective ways to establish "before rapport" with your audience.

DARREN'S BEFORE RAPPORT RITUAL

It's almost showtime in primetime, and you need to be fully focused on serving your audience. Darren says, "Skillset without mindset will leave your audience upset," and the last five minutes before you deliver your presentation is a critical time. This is when you need to connect to yourself. There are myriad ways to do this, including but not limited to prayer, meditation, a moment of silence, listening to music, and deep breathing. You will find your ritual.

Darren created a connection card that he keeps in his wallet with his four pre-primetime questions:

1. What is my intent?
2. Am I present?
3. Will I have fun?
4. How would I give this presentation if I knew it was my last one ever?

If these work for you, use them or create your own.

You have created version 1.0 of your unforgettable presentation. Now, commit to our process. Polishing and perfecting your presentation will take some time; however, the hard work is done. *Now, the fun begins.*

Check out examples of videos, introductions, and AV requirements on www.DeliverUnforgettablePresentations.com/Bonus.

COMMON MISTAKES

Mistake #1: Not internalizing the presentation.

Mistake #2: Not rehearsing enough.

Mistake #3: Not writing or creating the speech on paper.

Mistake #4: Not accepting feedback.

Mistake #5: Using a bio as an introduction.

Mistake #6: Not acknowledging and respecting the tech team.

Mistake #7: Not conducting a tech check.

STEP #7 ACTIVITY

Create your introduction.

Review your presentation and practice delivering your presentation alone. Then record your delivery to a test audience and assess it critically.

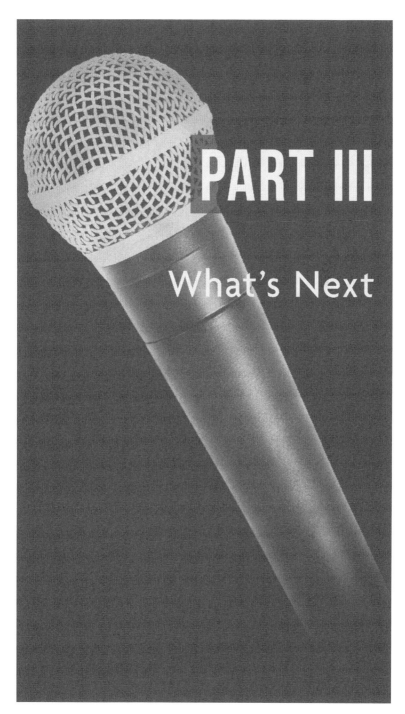

PART III

What's Next

How You Can Wow Your Audience In Virtual Presentations

BUSINESS AND EDUCATIONAL professionals, speakers, and trainers know that whenever you present, whether you're talking to one person or one hundred, you want to connect with your audience and get your message across. What's the best way to do this when you deliver a virtual presentation? Like it or not, virtual meetings and presentations are here to stay.

When designing and scripting your presentation, all the techniques you have learned from this book work in virtual presentations. Many professional speakers, your authors included, are perplexed when clients want us to deliver a virtual presentation for half our fee. Of course, we do not have to travel. However, virtual presentations are more stressful and less satisfying. They require more rehearsals, and we live in dread: "the technology will not work, and the internet may go down." And it often does. These elements add to the stress level of even the most seasoned of us.

Nothing happens without first understanding the technology.

Business entities use different technologies. They include Zoom, WebEx, GoToMeeting, and Teams. Conventions work with production companies and more sophisticated platforms. Even a seasoned presenter superb at delivering live presentations can find the shift nerve-racking.

Become familiar with your system and learn whatever platform you may have to use. Many are different than what you are used to. Request a technical demo with your client before the rehearsal of the presentation.

If you deliver from your home or office, make sure your environment is tidy behind you. If you use Zoom, you can upload background images that can be branded to your organization or the client's. However, you must have a green screen behind you. If you do not, you will often disappear into the background when you move.

Invest in a professional microphone to improve the sound.

Let there be light. Depending on the room, you will be best served if your window is in front of you. Depending on the time of day, that light changes. Invest in additional lights. The placement of the lights is important. We have all seen ring lights show up as demonic circles in our or other people's glasses.

Use a wired ethernet connection for best results. If you have a wireless connection and a large audience, you will have more problems.

Before you present, close every open program and application you are not using on your computer. Presenting virtually requires a large amount of bandwidth.

If you work from home, negotiate with family members to stay offline and not stream videos while you present.

Everything you do adds to or detracts from your message.

Tidy your background, or at least what your audience will see. Learn to make friends with your webcam, rather than looking down at your audience as you would in a meeting with team members.

Project energetic intimacy. Notch up your energy and get comfortable speaking to nobody. They are there; you just can't see them. If you find this difficult, bring a family member or friend into the room to be behind your computer and talk to them.

Always smile at the beginning of each content segment and when you pause, just as you would in person.

"Focus on your friends behind the lens."

MARK BROWN

With virtual presentations, you may need more slides with less content and even more variety than when you engage your audience live. Darren and Mark call these *pace elements*. These include your stories, questions, video clips, polls, Q & A, and virtual interaction via chat and emoticons.

When doing Q & A, we highly recommend you have a moderator who poses the questions to you. Make sure to ask for "short specific questions based on the ideas you have just heard." A moderator can combine and summarize and not ask questions off-topic. Always have a few questions prepared in case they are slow coming in.

If this is an important presentation, or you are getting paid to deliver it, you may want to consider going to a professional studio. They will have experienced videographers, multiple camera angles, green screens, studio lighting, great sound, and a teleprompter. You can use your slides, or they can add them after in post-production.

We hope this helps. Remember, virtual presentations are not going away.

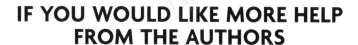

IF YOU WOULD LIKE MORE HELP FROM THE AUTHORS

✓ Check out Patricia's website at Fripp.com and her interactive online learning platform on Powerful, Persuasive Presentations at FrippVT. com. Patricia also coaches individuals and teams virtually and in person.

✓ Check out Darren's websites at StageTimeUniversity. com or StageTimeWorkshops.com.

✓ Learn how Mark can serve you or your team at markbrownspeaks.com.

✓ Check out examples of videos, introductions, and AV requirements on www. DeliverUnforgettablePresentations.com/Bonus.

✓ Watch examples of our professional keynote presentations to reinforce our process and help you create and constantly perfect your unforgettable presentation.

✓ Stay connected with us. If you are not yet a FrippVT member or a Stage Time University member, please consider joining us. Thank you for investing in your future and ours.

We look forward to meeting you at one of our events.

Looking Into The Future

"You need to master technique in order to abandon it."
Robert Fripp

ONGRATULATIONS, YOU JUST walked through a world-class presentation creation process based on decades of experience. Most presenters will never understand, to the deepest level, how to create a remembered and repeated presentation. Some will even spend their entire career trying to do it themselves and then wonder why they are average at best.

Think about it. Did you ever know someone who went to IKEA, bought a brand-new desk, brought it home, and assembled it without reading the instructions? Then they sit and wonder why there are two screws and a bracket left over. Just because you can get most of it right without the instructions doesn't mean you should. Missing one small piece can be the difference between just another presentation and an unforgettable one. This book is those instructions for assembling your presentation, and you don't need a screwdriver to do it.

Caution: You may feel overwhelmed now. It's normal. You are human. A world-class process can be too much to absorb at first. Both Mark and Darren had been professional presenters for years before learning the Fripp Presentation Model.

Some of the ideas you were presented may still not make complete sense. They will. We highly recommend that you go through this book again. Knowing the content is important, but when you internalize it, it becomes a part of you. You will be able to relax and enjoy more confidence and, at the same time, leave your audience better off. Each time you walk through the seven steps, it will make more and more sense. You will be able to create better presentations faster.

> **"When you shortcut the process, you shortcut the result."**
> DARREN LACROIX

Reminder: Anyone can deliver a presentation. The question is, will your presentation, on this day, to this audience, in this setting, be remembered and repeated? Why did you pick up this book in the first place? Why did you invest your time in this? No one becomes world-class overnight, but with a proven process, it is possible. The more effort you put into this process, the more powerful your presentations become.

Keep in mind every time you present, you have a tremendous responsibility. It is not just that one presentation. It is possibly your one chance to leave an indelible mark on your audience. Many of the people listening to you may never be in front of you again. This could be your one opportunity to influence them. Even though one presentation may not define your entire career, in their mind, it may be the first and last impression of you and your company. Every time you present, it can impact your career, reputation, and company's reputation. Make it count. You have in your hands the tools to help you deliver unforgettable presentations.

One more critical insight. Whether you are presenting to a small boardroom or a packed ballroom, your intention matters. Even if you know your content cold, check your mindset just before you present. Audiences these days are savvy. They've heard it all before, but they haven't heard you and your story. Even though they may sometimes be skeptical, they are open, especially if you need to stand out in your presentation.

Mark was advising Darren before he was to present in front of two thousand people. Darren felt the pressure. He needed to stand out from the competition. Mark noticed his ego was growing a bit. He pulled Darren aside and grounded him by saying, "You have the privilege to influence two thousand lives; what will you do with that opportunity?" Darren's mindset instantly shifted. He remembered why he was there. His mindset went from trying to stand out to trying to help. When you help people more than everyone else, you will stand out. Standing out is the side effect, not the direct intention. Intention matters. The audience can sense your intention because it is part of your delivery.

Consider this, "Skillset without mindset will leave your audience upset."

When your intention is right, and the audience can sense it, they will forgive many mistakes. They don't want you perfect; they want you present. Connect first and help them. Give them that perspective you worked hard to make simple and clear. When you take the time to make it clear, it becomes easier to know which points will best convince the jury in the audience's mind.

Remember to have fun. When you own the stage or the boardroom, it can be quite rewarding. When you have fun, they will too. Who wants to listen to a presenter who dreads their presentation, or worse, feels obligated to do it? It doesn't matter your subject. Have fun, and make it fun. Find a way. Humorous personal stories can make brilliant business points.

Yes, being unforgettable takes time and effort, but when you deliver unforgettable presentations, you become the presenter everyone loves. This gives you an unfair advantage in your career and opens the doors to more opportunities for you and your company. This goes beyond a single presentation on a single day; it becomes a multiplier.

APPENDIX

Acknowledgments

FROM **PATRICIA FRIPP.** Any success I have enjoyed results from a strong foundation and good values from a loving family. My father, Arthur Henry Fripp, told me on the first day I went to work, "Don't concentrate on making a lot of money. Concentrate on becoming the type of person others want to do business with, and you will most likely make a lot of money." My mother, Edie Fripp, or as my brother Robert calls her, "Saint Edith of the Valleys," told me, "Of course, it is the inner you that counts. However, you have to dress up and look good, so you can attract others who will then find out how smart and valuable you can be to them." Together, through their actions, they demonstrated "you can't be too kind or too generous." My parents also gave me the greatest gift of all, my brother Robert. Throughout our lives, we have been a constant support to each other. Robert is one of the most unforgettable guitarists and speakers you could ever hear.

My speaking career accelerated faster because of the help and encouragement of Mike Frank, who discovered me at my first National Speakers Association convention, and the late Bill Johnson. They were true supporters of women speakers. Certainly, my involvement with NSA has shortened my learning curve and resulted in many wonderful friends and opportunities.

I credit my speech coaches with helping me evolve into the career I now have. I'm especially grateful to the late Ron Arden, John Cantu, and Dawne Bernhardt.

Over the years, thousands of clients and audiences helped me perfect my craft and expand my business knowledge.

It has been said, "Friends are the family you choose." My cronies are numerous. I want to give a special shoutout to Diane Parente, Susan RoAne, Nancy Shina, and Carolina Girimonte.

From Wimborne Minster, a small town in Dorset in the south of England, to stages on five continents, it has been a heck of a ride. I feel as if I have more than gotten my money's worth.

From Darren LaCroix. To Mom and Dad, who despite telling them about my crazy, ridiculous dream that made no logical sense, loved me anyway. Thank you for allowing this broke dreamer, who had massive school loans and a business loan, but no business, to live at home and charge me next-to-nothing rent. Your unconditional love is what allowed me to pursue the seemingly impossible.

I would not be the speaker or person I am, if it were not for Patricia Fripp and Mark Brown. Thanks to my mentors along my journey, including Vinnie Favorito, Dave Fitzgerald, Rick Segel, and Rosemary Verri. And especially to my amazing team Regine Hollenbeck, Dawson Antonucci, Patti Marler, and Martina Krebsbach.

Also, thanks to Henry DeVries, Devin DeVries, Andy Baird, Lisa Haney, Edie DeVilbiss, Rich Hopkins, Paula Tomko, Tanya Murray, Manuela Braun Hendrickson, Liza Richards, Ashley Morris, and Katherine Wertheim.

From Mark Brown. To convert words delivered from physical and virtual world stages into written form is not as easy as one might think. On the contrary, it can be a daunting task, especially when coordinating one's efforts with the efforts of co-authors. So, how can I adequately thank my co-authors, Darren LaCroix and Patricia Fripp?

Darren has been my protégé, employer, co-presenter, collaborator, podcast co-host, friend, and brother for more than twenty years. He has endured my painful puns, and because he knows that I am a self-confessed word-nerd, he continues to subject himself to my nitpicky proofreading. The strength of our relationship has been, and continues to be, a blessing.

Patricia, whom I lovingly call "The inimitable Ms. Fripp," is a mentor, encourager, and guide par excellence. She was ready and willing to collaborate with Darren, other World Champion speakers, and me as the "Lady" of our "Lady and The Champs" events for more than a decade. Patricia was the first Certified Speaking Professional to invite me to share the platform at a National Speakers Association Chapter Meeting in Atlanta several years ago. She remains a guiding light, and I am forever in her debt.

My heartfelt thanks also go to our editor Henry DeVries and his team at Indie Books International. They adopted a professional eagle eye approach to this project, and their invaluable expertise was critical in making this book what it has become.

Any project of this magnitude requires sacrifices of energy and resources. Most important, however, is the investment of time for writing, editing, meetings, rewriting, more meetings, conference calls, and more. The cost for this time was paid by my best friend, my confidante, my inspiration, my biggest and most supportive fan, my partner in life, and my greatest gift from God, Andrea, my bride of almost forty years. The words, "I couldn't have done it without you" are often dismissed as cliché, but they are most appropriate here, and I do not offer them lightly. Thanks, Babe. I am among men most richly blessed!

About The Authors

PATRICIA FRIPP

Companies hire Patricia Fripp when they want to drive more business by polishing their sales conversations and presentations. Their leaders work with her to inspire action and build commitment through their words.

Patricia Fripp, CSP, CPAE, is a Hall of Fame keynote speaker, executive speech coach, and sales presentation and online learning expert. She was elected the first woman president of the National Speakers Association.

In Patricia's career, she has delivered over 3,500 presentations as well as hundreds of virtual presentations. Clients of her speech coaching include corporate leaders, technical and sales professionals, and seasoned professional speakers. Her online learning platform—FrippVT *Powerful, Persuasive Presentations*—is embraced as a "must-have" by speakers and companies worldwide.

Kiplinger's Personal Finance wrote, "Learning presentation skills from Patricia Fripp is one of the best ways to invest in you." She is the author of three books and co-author of another three. Patricia was named "One of the Top 30 Women in Sales" and "One of the Top 30 Global Gurus."

As a speechwriter, one of her speeches for a Johnson & Johnson executive was featured in *Vital Speeches of the Day* and won an Honorable Mention in the Cicero Speechwriting Awards.

When your message must be memorable, your presentation powerful, and your sales successful, Patricia Fripp can help.

DARREN LACROIX

Darren LaCroix's journey is a real-life underdog story filled with humor and hope.

After a failed business in 1992, Darren took a dare and went on stage at an open-mic night at a Boston comedy club. He bombed miserably. It was horrible. The headliner that night told him to "keep your day job, kid." Friends told him that his dream of making people laugh for a living was crazy and stupid. He didn't listen.

He may have been born without a funny bone in his body, but Darren possessed the desire to learn and the willingness to fail. This self-proclaimed student of comedy is living proof that *anything* can be learned.

Less than nine years later, in 2001, Darren outspoke 25,000 contestants from fourteen countries to become the World Champion of Public Speaking. Ironically, it was with a funny speech. Some said it was one of the best speeches in the history of the contest.

Since that victory, he has delivered keynotes in every state in the United States and forty-four international cities. He is passionate about showing people that if you pray, find the right mentors, and become a sponge, anything is possible.

Darren is currently the only speaker in the world who is a CSP (Certified Speaking Professional), an AS (Accredited Speaker), and a World Champion of Public Speaking. Despite this, Darren always reminds people, "The letters after your name are not as important as the professional you become in the process."

He is the co-host of the *Unforgettable Presentations* podcast. Through his live workshops and StageTimeUniversity. com, he helps good presenters become *unforgettable*.

MARK BROWN

Mark Brown is a Certified Speaking Professional who helps people overcome their fears to reach their maximum potential and achieve ever-increasing levels of excellence.

Originally from Kingston, Jamaica, Mark immigrated to the United States at eighteen with only forty dollars in his pocket and a dream for a better life. Fifteen years later, he won the 1995 World Championship of Public Speaking and has since delivered more than 3,500 presentations to more than 1.7 million people on five continents.

Mark has been featured in the *New York Times* and on CNN Headline News and even had his own Emmy-nominated PBS Special, *Words Count – with Mark Brown.*

A frequent presenter at National Speakers Association meetings and keynote speaker at Toastmasters International Conferences worldwide, Mark has shared his insights across various industries, including finance, education, hospitality, transportation, marketing, and technology.

He is the co-author of the book *The Speaker's Edge* and co-host of the weekly *Unforgettable Presentations* podcast.

He lives in Lizella, Georgia, with Andrea, his wife of almost forty years.

Imagine the results you would receive if everyone perceived you as a
Powerful, Persuasive Presenter.

You can be. Easily, quickly, conveniently, and cost-effectively.

FrippVT (Virtual Training) will help you perfect all aspects of public speaking and business communications 24/7. Highly interactive. Learn at your own speed.

"The information in FrippVT is as valuable as any college course I've taken. This is a resource that everyone needs. **The investment is worth ten times more than I paid and has been life-changing.** *My fees, recommendations, and referrals have increased dramatically. For the first time in my speaking career, I know exactly want I am doing when I walk on stage. One technique in course 11 helped me win an international presentation."*

– Mitzi Perdue,
Author of How to Make Your Family Business Last

Want to sound more confident, influential and credible? Take the free trial.
www.frippvt.com/free-trial-offer

Patricia FRIPP
pfripp@fripp.com • www.fripp.com • (415) 753-6556

Made in United States
Troutdale, OR
12/13/2024

26145391R00082